'Nita Menezes' *Be Financially Smart: A Modern Woman's Guide to Money* is an indispensable resource that offers clear, actionable guidance for women to take control of their financial futures. With her extensive experience, Nita presents practical strategies that every woman can apply. This book is a must-read for women determined to achieve financial empowerment and for men who support the financial education of the women in their lives.'

**—Dr Swati Lodha, Author and Director,
MET Institute of Management**

'The reasons why Indian women are financially illiterate are rooted in several historical, social, economic, religious and psychological factors. But now is the time to change that. What I particularly like about this book is that it's not theoretical gyan, but a practical guide that has emerged out of author's personal experience, ably supported by others' real-life examples. Don't just read this excellent contribution; DO it to transform your life.

**—Prof. Arun Patil, Dean, MET Asian Management
Development Centre**

'Nita Menezes, a strong advocate for financial education for all, especially children and women, has crafted a well-thought-out, all-inclusive book that provides strategies and tools ready to be put into action. Dive in, become financially smart and grab your copy now. I am excited about the possibilities this book offers, and I am confident you will be too.'

**—Fatema Agarkar, Chairperson and Founder,
Agarkar Centre of Excellence**

'In *Be Financially Smart: A Modern Woman's Guide to Money*, Nita Menezes transforms complex financial concepts into a relatable and empowering guide. This book is not just about financial literacy; it's a call to action for women to take control of their financial futures with confidence and clarity. A must-read for anyone seeking to build a secure and prosperous life.'

—Vaibhav Manek, Co-founder and Partner, KNAV

'Women possess a remarkable knack for saving every penny, no matter their situation. Nita's book acknowledges that and teaches them to channel this expertise in the right direction for them to become financially literate and be smarter with their money.'
—**Tarun Katial, Founder and CEO, coto**

'Nita Menezes' book *Be Financially Smart: A Modern Woman's Guide to Money* is an invaluable resource that empowers women with the financial insights and strategies they need to succeed. With nearly three decades of experience in the financial industry, Nita has crafted a guide that is both comprehensive and accessible. Highly recommended for fostering financial empowerment and prudence.'
—**Dr Nandita Mishra, Director, CIMR**

'By sharing real-life stories of women who have overcome financial challenges, Nita has made the subject more accessible and relatable, breaking down complex concepts into understandable and inspiring narratives. This book is a valuable resource that will undoubtedly benefit thousands of women across the country, enabling them to become financially smart and independent. Together we can.'
—**Dr Harbeen Arora Rai, Founder and President, G100 |All Ladies League (ALL) | Women Economic Forum (WEF) |WICCI, Women's Indian Chamber of Commerce and Industry |SHEconomy**

BE FINANCIALLY SMART

Nita Menezes is a respected thought leader, keynote speaker and the founder of Financially Smart and MoneyPrastha. With almost three decades of expertise, she is a Certified Financial Planner and has a Fellowship in Life Insurance. Nita serves as the national president of WICCI Financial Literacy & Management Council and the India Country Chair for G100 Club—Financial Empowerment.

Driven by her passion for financial literacy, Nita strives to impact one million lives globally. She offers diverse online courses such as 'My Financial Freedom Blueprint', 'Financially Smart Young Adults' and 'Financially Empowered Woman', along with interactive offline and online workshops for teenagers, women and educational institutions. She conducts curated workshops for both corporates and the public. Through mentoring, she simplifies complexities, empowering clients and students to make smart life choices.

She is appointed as a Professor of Practice by Sanjivani Group of Institutes for Personal Financial Management. Nita also designs curriculums on personal finance for various streams, including management, medical and engineering colleges.

Nita is also a certified image consultant and specialises in personal branding and influence for financial entrepreneurs.

Additionally, she has contributed to various articles in magazines like *Outlook, FPSB India*, etc. and has co-authored the book *Know your Finance* in collaboration with WICCCI FLM & Research Foundation of India with her team of WICCI women.

She shares valuable insights on social media, balancing her dedication to health and wealth through fitness activities, reading and travelling with her family.

Explore more about Nita at www.nitamenezes.com and her firm at www.financiallysmart.in and www.moneyprastha.com.

Connect on social media via linktr.ee/bfinanciallysmart or write to Nita at finsmartwomen@gmail.com.

Praise for *Be Financially Smart*

'Financial literacy is the cornerstone of empowerment. Financial literacy leads to financial independence and mindful expenditure—both essential for a higher quality of life for both men and women. Today, society and stereotypes are changing and making way for a more progressive investment culture, encouraging women to take the lead. I believe women undergo different life experiences which differ in their perspective towards investments—they can go from managing home budgets to being smart investors. Books like *Be Financially Smart: A Modern Woman's Guide to Money* are important to educate, equip and empower women with added knowledge and tools needed to take charge of their financial lives.'

—Arundhati Bhattacharya, CEO and Chairperson, Salesforce India

'By merging their natural talents with formal education in financial planning, women can spearhead the movement towards a prosperous future for themselves and their communities. In *Be Financially Smart: A Modern Woman's Guide to Money*, Nita Menezes delves into these themes, offering invaluable insights and practical advice to empower women to take control of their financial destiny. This book is an essential read for every woman aspiring to achieve financial independence and shape a brighter future.

—Krishan Mishra, CEO, FPSB India

'I am so glad that Nita Menezes has addressed the issue of financial empowerment for women in her book with practical examples and templates that people, particularly women, can use. I am sure *Be Financially Smart: A Modern Woman's Guide to Money* is going to be a bestseller.'

—Malavika R. Harita, Teacher, mentor, communication evangelist and brand strategist

NITA MENEZES

BE FINANCIALLY SMART

THE MODERN WOMAN'S GUIDE TO MONEY

Published by Westland Business, an imprint of Westland Books, a division of Nasadiya Technologies Private Limited, in 2024

No. 269/2B, First Floor, 'Irai Arul', Vimalraj Street, Nethaji Nagar, Alapakkam Main Road, Maduravoyal, Chennai 600095

Westland, the Westland logo, Westland Business and the Westland Business logo are the trademarks of Nasadiya Technologies Private Limited, or its affiliates.

Copyright © Nita Menezes, 2024

Nita Menezes asserts the moral right to be identified as the author of this work.

ISBN: 9789360452223

10 9 8 7 6 5 4 3 2 1

The views and opinions expressed in this work are the author's own and the facts are as reported by her, and the publisher is in no way liable for the same.

All rights reserved

Typeset by Mukul

Printed at Thomson Press (India) Ltd

No part of this book may be reproduced, or stored in a retrieval system, or transmitted in any form or by any means, electronic, mechanical, photocopying, recording, or otherwise, without express written permission of the publisher.

This book is dedicated to all you women out there of all ages, and to the supportive men who stand by them, believing in their dreams and empowering them to achieve greatness.

Contents

Contents

Contents

Section 5
Mastering Financial Resilience and Empowerment

Section 6
Navigating Challenges, Empowering Lives

Contents

Foreword

As we navigate through an era marked by rapid change and unprecedented challenges, the importance of financial literacy, especially among women, cannot be overstated. It is with great pleasure that I introduce *Be Financially Smart: A Modern Woman's Guide to Money* by Nita Menezes. This book is not just a guide but can be an inspiration for women seeking to empower themselves through financial knowledge.

In my role as CEO, I have witnessed first hand the transformative power of financial literacy in the mutual fund industry and steered my company to be at the forefront of investor education. It equips individuals with the tools they need to make informed decisions, plan for their futures and navigate the complexities of today's economic landscape. This book addresses these needs with clarity and practicality, offering actionable insights that are as relevant to seasoned professionals as they are to those just beginning their financial journey.

Nita Menezes has crafted a comprehensive resource that demystifies the world of finance. From understanding the basics of money management to exploring advanced investment strategies, this guide covers it all. It is particularly commendable for its focus on the unique financial challenges and opportunities that women face, providing tailored advice to help them achieve financial independence and security.

Be Financially Smart is more than a book; it is a call to action, as is rightly put. It encourages women to take control of their financial destinies and offers the knowledge and confidence needed to do so. As you delve into its pages, I am confident that you will find the inspiration and guidance required to transform your financial life.

With this foreword, I endorse the effort of Nita Menezes and urge every reader to embrace the wisdom within. Let this book be your companion on the path to financial empowerment.

Sincerely,

A. Balasubramanian
Managing Director and CEO,
Aditya Birla Sun Life AMC Ltd

A Call to Action

'The future belongs to those who believe in the beauty of their dreams.'

—Eleanor Roosevelt

IN A WORLD WHERE FINANCIAL LITERACY IS THE ARMOUR, 'Be Financially Smart' emerges as the rallying cry for change. Join me on a journey that transcends mere awareness and dives deep into the waters of financial empowerment—a journey that is not just a book but a mission, a revolution.

Financial literacy is not just a choice; it is the very foundation of a happy, healthy and wealthy nation. Yet, the global survey reveals a stark truth: despite comprising 20% of the world's population, only 27% of India's populace is financially literate, with a staggering 80% of women grappling with financial illiteracy.[1] The repercussions are profound, as many women find themselves entangled in unfortunate situations due to a lack of knowledge, often leading to unexpected financial ruin.

Having weathered the storms of my own financial missteps and witnessed the struggles of those around me, I can say this book is not just a compilation of wisdom but a testament to the pressing need for financial literacy. For nearly three decades, I have been a guide, mentor and witness to the financial lives of individuals and families, realising that financial literacy is not just about investments—it's about transforming every facet of a woman's life.

Through the lens of significant events like demonetisation and the recent global pandemic, the resilience and saving prowess of women has emerged clearly. Many women from humble households were found to be holding significant sums in cash that no one knew about, and this illustrates their financial acumen. The pandemic underscored the importance of savings and investments, proving that financial literacy is not determined by gender, age or circumstance.

This book is not just a guide; it's a blueprint for becoming financially smart. Each chapter draws from real-life stories and experiences, offering actionable steps for beginners, DIY enthusiasts, students and financial advisors. It extends beyond financial literacy, delving into areas crucial to a woman's life, empowering her to make informed choices and navigate life's challenges.

---

1 'Survey Report - Rating agency Standard & Poor's (S&P) - S&P Global FinLit Survey - https://gflec.org/initiatives/sp-global-finlit-survey/ and NCFE & SEBI recent survey https://old.ncfe.org.in/images/pdfs/annual_reports/Annual_Report_2022-23.pdf

A Call to Action

This book is a call to action, urging women to not merely be aware but to be alert and updated, equipped with the tools needed to make smart and informed decisions.

So, dear women, are you ready to embark on this transformative journey? If you dream of a stress-free, happy lifestyle and have the desire to make smart, informed choices daily, you've chosen the right path. Grab your favourite beverage and a notebook and find a serene spot. This is not just a book; it's your guide to financial success and a stress-free lifestyle. The aim of this book and our course, 'Financially SMART Woman' is to make this transformation as easy as possible for you.

Visit www.financiallysmart.in for ongoing updates and access to valuable information. Join my workshops and online courses designed to guide you through becoming a financially smart woman.

Imagine a life where you hold the knowledge and tools to make informed financial decisions. This book is your key to that reality—a reality where you not only survive but thrive.

With gratitude,
—Nita

Introduction

'The journey of a thousand miles begins with one step.'
—Lao Tzu

My Story, My Purpose, My Why

BEFORE WE DIVE IN … LET ME TELL YOU A LITTLE BIT ABOUT MYSELF, why I got into this profession, and my WHY behind writing this book.

A yellow hair dryer was the reason I changed my career path. Surprised … Let me tell you why?

I was born into a traditional middle-class family of two daughters, with my dad being the only key earning member. My mom quit working when my sister and I were born and became a homemaker. She was awesome at saving, and thanks to her, I started earning and saving from an early age. However, we had no proper plan or strategy for our finances. The only place I was aware of where my dad invested his money was in banks through savings and fixed deposits or corporate/company deposits. We had limited knowledge and never explored any other avenues. We were aware that saving is very important, but never thought about the growth of money or had the slightest clue how our money can make us more money. The focus was to generate income through a salary or through freelance work to take care of expenses and save the remaining.

In 1992, a yellow hair dryer—yes, I still remember the colour—changed the course of my career. It was the most expensive gift I had received at the time, offered as an additional incentive by an investment scheme that promised quick and high returns. Lured by this enticing bonus, I invested my hard-earned money, only to later discover that the scheme was a Ponzi scheme. A Ponzi scheme is an investment scam that pays early investors with money taken from later investors, thus creating an illusion of large profits. It promises a high rate of return with little risk to the investor and relies on word-of-mouth, as new investors hear about the big returns earned by early investors. This seemingly lucrative opportunity turned out to be a costly mistake. My dad was introduced to this scheme through a friend, and as he was investing most of his retirement funds, I invested some part of my money too, as this money was lying in an FD account. Lack of knowledge and awareness and being financially illiterate taught me my first and very important life lesson.

I was devastated as it was my hard-earned money and it had all gone. I was left with the yellow hair dryer and some post-dated cheques that failed to encash. Not just my dad and me, but many other people had invested their life savings and investments, including their retirement funds, in this scheme.

And that's how I found my WHY, my purpose. Since then, I decided to find out the reason my dad and many more people like him continue to fail to see some of the obvious red flags and why they failed to protect their lifetime savings from a fraudulent scheme without doing the necessary homework.

For almost three decades now, I have been helping people manage their financial lives. I have worked with a couple of firms, met many clients from different professional backgrounds and worked with many families too.

This book is a result of three decades of experiences as any other woman who is a daughter, wife, daughter-in-law, mother, financial consultant and mentor trying to understand and demystify this crazy yet very important thing called money. If you have trouble living within your means or struggle to find the right balance between saving and spending, you're not alone. I have been there myself, made a couple of mistakes, rectified them and have also observed many of my clients' fears and frustrations around money. I have been their sounding board and guided and hand-held them through testing times.

After being in the industry for a few years, I observed most women took a back seat time and again when it came to financial decisions. Most of them would shy away from participating in family financial decisions either due to some fear, lack of interest or just because it was considered taboo for the woman to talk about money in their family.

I penned this book to help you not just by creating awareness about investments, but also with the objective to focus and address every area of a woman's life whilst providing valuable guidance. It's truly been life-changing not only for my women clients but their families and for myself as well.

People often come to me seeking advice on how to invest their money. They ask me which mutual funds are the best, what stocks will yield the best returns, where they should invest and even whether they should invest in cryptocurrencies like Bitcoin. They also ask me if they should invest in particular traditional or unit-linked life insurance products and if they can give up their individual health coverage as they feel they have been paying for years and not used it till date. As a financial expert, they believe I hold the secret to building wealth.

But when I start asking them questions, such as these:

- Have you created an emergency/contingency fund?
- Are you aware of your cashflows and your net worth?
- Do you have debt?
- How did you decide on the amount of life cover you need?
- Have you written down and set SMART goals?
- What is the rate of return needed to help you achieve your goals?
- Do you have adequate health cover for all the family members?

They seem entirely clueless. I often find that they are lacking in basic financial knowledge. Many of them are unaware of the importance of having an emergency fund or making sure their investments are inflation-proof.

Through my experience, I have learnt that financial empowerment is not just about investing in the right stocks or mutual funds or buying a life insurance policy. It is about giving women the knowledge and skills to take charge of their financial lives.

That is why I authored this book. I want to guide every aspect of a woman's financial life, from setting SMART goals and managing debt to building an emergency fund and making smart investment decisions. I stress the importance of having adequate insurance coverage and ways to make investments inflation-proof.

My approach is not about giving you a magic formula to become rich overnight but, rather, helping you understand the basic principles of personal finance and how to apply them to your life. Every woman can become financially empowered, regardless of her income level or educational background.

If you're ready to take control of your financial life and become a financially smart woman, this book is for you. I hope the tips and strategies I've shared will help you build a solid financial foundation and achieve your financial goals. Remember, financial freedom is not just about money. It's about having the freedom to do what you love and love what you do.

Being a Financially SMART Woman in Turbulent Times

It was the first week of June 2020, a time of great uncertainty, confusion and panic across India due to the sudden rise of COVID-19 cases and the announcement of a nationwide lockdown. It was around 11.40 p.m. when I received an SOS text from my college friend Sheena Shetty. She wanted to know if we could get on a call ASAP, as it was an emergency.

Sheena was one of the brightest students in our class, and we all looked up to her. She was smart, organised and focused. She was among the top retail professionals, looking after one of the premier retail brands in India and doing extremely well in her career. We had caught up over coffee a couple of years back after we bumped into each other at our college reunion in 2015. That's where she shared that she was doing very well in life and that her career was at its peak. Her husband was managing a holiday resort they owned, and life was set. As we sipped some hot coffee and relived our college days, we had a brief talk on my profession as a financial coach, and I shared my thoughts and experiences of women who are successful in their career but don't take interest in managing their money. That's when we discussed about the importance of being financially informed and financially literate, and I asked Sheena if she had a handle on her financial life. She promptly replied that most working corporate women like her were empowered because they had a good income and were sorted as they had a life partner who was a finance expert. She believed that she didn't need to worry and take on any additional stress but work hard for a few more years until she decided to enjoy a luxurious lifestyle at the resort they owned. Not wanting to be pushy and realising she was happy and content, I told her we should catch up sometime again and talk more on this subject. After that we both got busy in our professional and family life and just connected off and on via text messages and wishing each other on birthdays.

When I received her SOS text late that night, I was surprised and dialled back immediately. Sheena broke down over the phone—she said she was unable to sleep the last few nights and was confused and scared. She could not think of anyone better to speak to. She shared how her world had suddenly come to a standstill, and she was not prepared for it. She had lost her husband a couple of weeks back and she needed someone trustworthy whom she could talk to.

Due to the pandemic, Sheena's company had laid off a lot of people, and she was politely informed that her services were not needed any more by her employer a couple of months back. Her husband Tarun had invested all their money in stocks, derivatives and commodities. He had parked a big sum in some multi-bagger stocks that he believed would do well based on his research and parked some funds in cryptocurrency too. He had taken out some huge loans for the expansion of his hotel business and the resort facilities, and most of the income was being redirected there. With the pandemic setting in, the EMIs and salaries of the staff continued, but there was no income as the hotel rooms were going empty, and the lockdown was announced with no clarity over when it would end.

The family was already going through a tough time when Tarun suffered a brain haemorrhage while returning from work. He was admitted to the ICU for a week but did not come back to consciousness due to some other health complications and passed away a week later. Amidst the pandemic, it was a task to release his body from the hospital authorities, and they had to do the final rites out there.

Sheena was suddenly faced with a situation amid grief, holding herself strong for her kids and family and not knowing what to expect and from where to begin. Her husband had just passed away, leaving her alone to deal with the aftermath of his financial decisions. As she poured out her heart over the next hour, I listened in shock, realising that this could happen to anyone, even those who seem to have it all together.

Sheena's husband had not taken sufficient life insurance coverage, and the policies he did have were not enough to cover their debts. Moreover, he had not opted for the Married Women Property Act in his insurance policies (What's the MWP Act? I will be sharing more about this later.) The creditors were quick to recover what they could, leaving Sheena with little to fall back on.

To make matters worse, his hospitalisation expenses had exhausted the meagre health insurance floater cover of 5 lakhs that they had between them, leaving her with astronomical medical bills from his hospital stay, for which she had to dip into her gratuity funds. The group mediclaim cover that was offered by her previous employer had also stopped with her exit from the company, so she was left with no health cover at the moment.

Every day was a surprise when she found out about the money they owed to creditors, the interest piling up and understood more about their business.

They had no long-term revenue-generating assets and very few assets that could be immediately converted to cash (liquid assets) but had a lot of illiquid assets like real estate and land, and liabilities like loans. They had also invested their money in some high-risk investments like derivatives, commodities and cryptocurrency, and Sheena had no understanding of them as they were all handled by Tarun. She was only aware of her salary, most of which was used to maintain her own lifestyle expenses, which covered her own shopping, travel and outings with friends.

As I sat there listening to her story, I couldn't help but feel guilty for not pushing her to be more involved in the family's financial decisions. I had assumed that her husband had everything under control, and Sheena seemed content to let him handle it all. But now, I realised how wrong I was.

Together, Sheena and I spent the next few months untangling the financial mess left behind by her husband's passing. It was a Herculean task, but we managed to get most of the things if not all in order and settle the debts slowly but surely.

Reflecting on Sheena's story, I knew I had to do more to help other women take charge of their financial lives. I started writing a book, creating online courses and organising workshops and panel discussions to spread financial literacy and empowerment among women. I decided to spearhead and founded our community of women—Women India Chamber of Commerce & Industry for Financial Literacy & Management (WICCI FLM) Council, G100 Mission Million for Financial Empowerment—with the aim to make a meaningful difference in the financial wellness space by sharing real-life stories of women and encouraging them to take charge of their financial lives.

Sheena's story is a cautionary tale that emphasises the need for financial literacy and preparedness. None of us know what the future holds, but we can take steps to be ready for whatever comes our way. By investing time in ourselves and making informed choices, we can ensure a better future for ourselves and our families.

Section 1

Let's Have Some Honest Conversations

Money is a topic often shrouded in secrecy and taboo, especially in Indian households where traditional beliefs and practices have relegated women to the periphery of financial discussions. In many cultures, Goddess Lakshmi is revered as the epitome of wealth and prosperity. She symbolises abundance, fortune and well-being. However, paradoxically, the very societies that invoke her blessings often exclude women from actively participating in financial decisions. This lack of inclusion has perpetuated a complex relationship with money, leaving women unprepared and unaware of how to manage their finances. However, this is not just true in India or in a particular culture or society but globally as well.

In the Indian cultural landscape, discussing money, budgets and financial planning openly has been a rarity. Women and children, in particular, have often been shielded from these conversations, leading to a significant gap in financial literacy. The prevailing belief that 'a man is a financial plan' or that financial control should be surrendered to someone else, typically a male member, has further discouraged women from taking charge of their financial lives.

The truth is, at some point in their lives, women will be faced with making financial decisions. Whether in times of joy or sorrow, being unaware and unprepared can be a daunting prospect. The prevalent notion that financial decisions are solely a man's responsibility is both outdated and detrimental. It's time for women to challenge these stereotypes, as waiting for someone else to take control may lead to regrets in critical situations.

Being afraid or having doubts about financial matters is natural, but it's never too late to take charge of your financial life. 'If it is to BE … it is up to ME.' Acknowledging fear and doubt is the first step; the key lies in applying the knowledge acquired. In a society where women have been kept in the dark about finances, gaining knowledge becomes the catalyst for empowerment.

Life is unpredictable, and financial challenges can arise unexpectedly. Whether it's job loss, illness or unforeseen circumstances, being prepared is the key. Women must equip themselves with the knowledge and information necessary to navigate these challenges seamlessly, without relying solely on someone else.

A recent survey reveals a stark contrast in financial literacy between India and developed nations. Only 27% of adults in India are considered financially literate, compared to 67% in the UK, 59% in Singapore and 64% in the US.[2] This gap highlights the pressing need for improved financial education and awareness in the Indian context.

In India, mismanagement and mis-selling by some banking and financial professionals have contributed to a lack of trust. Instances of selling risky products under the guise of free financial advice have left many individuals wary and hesitant. This has led to a state of analysis paralysis,

---

2 'S&P Global Finlit Survey', *Global Financial Literacy Excellence Center*, https://gflec.org/initiatives/sp-global-finlit-survey/.

where the fear of being deceived hinders proactive financial decision-making.

Many individuals, including the younger generation, fall into the trap of personal loan and credit card debts without understanding the repercussions. Unchecked spending, accumulating multiple loans and missing payments create a vicious cycle known as the 'Debt Trap'. Lack of basic financial skills and literacy contributes significantly to this widespread issue.

An alarming revelation from a survey conducted shares that approximately 50% of the Indian population resorts to borrowing from informal sources.[3] This lack of awareness leads to individuals paying higher interest rates than necessary, highlighting the critical need for financial education to guide them towards formal and affordable financial channels.

Both in urban and rural settings, women often invest in chit fund schemes rather than safer options through banks, resulting in substantial financial losses. Lack of understanding about safer investment instruments and a reliance on informal financial practices demonstrate the urgent necessity of financial literacy.

Education becomes paramount to break the cycle of financial ignorance. Integrating financial literacy into the school and college curriculum is essential. By equipping individuals with the necessary financial knowledge and tools from an early age, the transition from their learning years into their earning years can happen seamlessly giving them a great head start into their financial lives.

---

3 Rajesh Shukla, Prabir Kumar Ghosh hind Rachna Sharma, 'Assessing the Effectiveness of Small Borrowing in India', *Centre for Macro Consumer Research*, 2011.

Studies reveal that women worry more than men about financial security. The stress of making ends meet, coupled with the fear of losing everything, is prevalent. Honest conversations about money are crucial to alleviate this burden and empower women to take control of their financial destinies.

Observing family dynamics, it becomes evident that more women tend to outlive men. Factors like marrying older men, taking breaks for family responsibilities and higher life expectancy require women to be more proactive in financial planning. The need to save, invest and plan for a longer period becomes imperative for women's financial well-being.

It's time to dismantle the barriers surrounding money conversations, especially for women. This chapter encourages an honest dialogue about the crucial tool we possess—money. By addressing financial literacy, debunking myths and embracing empowerment, women can redefine their relationship with money. Let's collectively change the narrative, fostering a culture where financial conversations are not just welcomed but celebrated.

In the upcoming chapters, we will delve deeper into practical steps for financial empowerment, guiding women on the path to financial freedom and security.

Why Money Is Not the Goal but Is an Important Tool

'Money is a tool. It will take you wherever you wish, but it will not replace you as the driver.'

—Ayn Rand

OUR LIFE IS THE SUM OF ALL THE DECISIONS WE TAKE DAILY, AND IF WE are able to take smart and informed decisions daily, can you imagine how stress-free our life can be? Many of our decisions revolve around money too. If you want to learn about money, you first need to understand what money really is and the role it plays in your life.

The importance of money is clear when you factor in all the costs that are needed for maintaining a sustainable and healthy lifestyle. Money has no value on its own. It just serves as a medium of exchange.

As Ayn Rand writes, money is important as a tool—it can help you achieve your goals and what you desire provided you are in charge, as it cannot replace you. Money is just a tool because, on its own, it can benefit nothing. However, with it, we can acquire something of value to our lives and that of others. It isn't the goal, it's the means of achieving goals. It isn't the end, it's a means to an end.

Think about it. When you have stacks of money piled up in the house, what can they do? Nothing. Like a book sitting on your bookshelf, money can't provide any value unless it is put to some use. Just as a book becomes beneficial when you start reading it and apply what you have learnt from it, money becomes beneficial when directed where the value is.

Money is neither bad nor good. It is neutral. But when you start using it, it gets its value. So having a goal of having ₹1 crore in the bank is okay. *But why?* The 1 crore is just a pretty big tool that can facilitate many things. However, when this tool is used effectively and we as the drivers decide and plan the course and act accordingly, it can help you lead a stress-free, happy, healthy and wealthy lifestyle. At the end of the day, this is the most important thing that anyone ever wants, isn't it?

Let's quickly review some of the significant moments in your life: graduation, marriage, starting a business, starting a family, moving and so on. Consider this: did you get married, attend school or build a business simply because you could afford it? No. You pursued these milestones to achieve specific life goals: finding a life partner, earning a degree and owning a company.

Most of the time, people think about money as one of their 'big' moments or goals when it simply is just a small part of what helps them get there. So, what does this tell you? Money is not a goal or moment in your life; instead, it's a vehicle to reach your goals.

We also need to understand what role money plays in our lives.

We all want to be happy, but we all know that money alone can't buy you happiness. However, it surely is a particularly important factor as it can be a means to bring you happiness. Financial well-being is important if you want to provide for your family's basic needs. Money can buy security and safety for your loved ones. We need money to take care of our health, for our food and for a good education.

Money is great to have, fun to spend and, for some of us, hard to keep. Everyone is different. Your relationship with money depends largely on your upbringing. Your feelings for money may be connected to happiness, security, anxiety, confidence...

You also have habits and attitudes that have been shaped by your family. A child whose parents talk with ease about family finances will think differently about money than a girl whose parents worry or argue when the bills arrive. A girl who has grown up seeing her mother saving in a disciplined manner will have different spending habits than a girl who has only seen her mother spending all her money.

All this means that your feelings about money may be complicated, but the way you use money doesn't have to be....

Hence, it is important to remember that money is a tool and not a goal. Money that is invested through investment products like mutual funds, stocks, etc. are the vehicles to help you reach your goal.

Having thought through money and its role in our lives, it is time we examine our unique relationship with money.

Understanding your WHY

For some, money embodies security, while for others, it symbolises freedom or luxury. The first step towards financial empowerment is understanding our WHY. Yet, many women grapple with ingrained money messages from their past, perpetuated by societal norms. Messages like 'Leave financial decisions to men', or the guilt associated with spending on personal needs, have lingered for too long. Because of this conditioning, they hesitate to ask themselves this important question and to prioritise their own WHY, often ceding space to the motivations of others, such as their family or spouse.

It's not just a local woe; it's a global phenomenon. Women, from homemakers to senior finance executives, share a common struggle—a reluctance to manage money and make independent financial decisions. History, however, stands as a testament to women's exceptional saving prowess and their ability to manage households effectively.

It's time to shed these outdated money messages and discover our purpose. To be a financially smart woman is not merely about gaining knowledge; it's about actionable steps and taking control of our financial destinies.

The truth is, spending money is easy—especially in a world perpetually tempting us with products and experiences. Yet, many women find themselves ensnared in this vicious cycle, grappling with money worries throughout their lives. The key lies not just in acquiring knowledge but in acting upon it.

Knowledge, when acted upon, becomes power. Confidence alone doesn't equate to competence. Women often grapple with mental barriers, fearing mistakes or questioning financial decisions. It's time to challenge these barriers, learn from mistakes and not shy away from questioning.

As we embark on this journey, let's collectively dismantle the fear surrounding money. It's a tool—a means to an end. This is an invitation to overcome challenges, seek help when needed, and remember that asking is the first step toward receiving. It's time to break the glass ceiling, take charge and get financially smart.

A pervasive anxiety about money shadows many lives, yet it doesn't have to be the norm. Money is a tool, not a source of fear. By adopting a new perspective, engaging in open financial conversations and seeking assistance when needed, you can dissipate the fear surrounding money.

Let's delve into Meera's story—an inspiring journey of resilience and determination that dispels the myths surrounding money and fear. Meera, a high-ranking official known for her honesty and integrity, harboured a deep-seated belief that money was inherently evil. Despite her professional prowess, this fear of money permeated every aspect of her life, influencing her financial decisions and causing her to shy away from managing her finances.

Life took an unexpected turn for Meera when her husband suffered a severe paralytic attack . Overnight, she became the sole provider, caring for her ailing husband and two young children. Thrust into the role of the family's financial anchor, Meera realised her aversion to managing money was no longer sustainable. The heavy responsibility of providing for her family forced her to confront her fears and take control of her financial destiny.

Thus began Meera's journey of financial self-discovery. Starting from scratch, she dedicated herself to learning the fundamentals of financial management. She immersed herself in books, sought guidance from financial experts and embraced every opportunity to expand her financial literacy. Through perseverance and determination, Meera gradually transformed her relationship with money.

As she gained confidence in her financial abilities, Meera began to see money not as a source of evil, but as a tool for empowerment and security. She learnt to save diligently, invest wisely and manage her finances effectively to secure a better future for herself and her family. Her journey from fear to financial empowerment was not easy, but Meera's resilience and determination propelled her forward.

Today, Meera stands as a shining example of overcoming the fear of money and dispelling the myths surrounding its perceived evils. Not only has she become financially savvy in her own right, but she has also become a mentor to others seeking to navigate the complex world of finance. Her story serves as a beacon of hope for women everywhere, inspiring them to confront their fears, take charge of their finances and build a brighter future for themselves and their families.

As you step into the realm of investing, remember, it's not about the thrill of the moment; it's about creating a life of abundance. This too shall pass, and the power to shape your financial destiny is in your hands. It's time to break free from the shackles, seize control and embark on a journey of financial empowerment.

CHAPTER 2

Unravelling the Psychology of Money

'The real measure of your wealth is how much you'd be worth if you lost all your money.'

—Anonymous

THE RELATIONSHIP BETWEEN WOMEN AND MONEY HAS LONG BEEN influenced by societal conditioning and deep-rooted patriarchal norms. Yet, the moment is ripe for women to redefine this narrative—they must dismantle the traditional barriers and construct a dynamic alliance with their finances, a connection grounded in empowerment, equality and financial autonomy.

Money, a word that resonates differently with each of us, holds the power to shape our dreams, fears and aspirations. Our individual passions, fears and dreams colour the canvas of our financial perspectives. Understanding the psychology of money becomes key to unlocking our unique thoughts, emotions and behaviours surrounding it.

Exploring the psychology of money is like peeling back the layers of our financial mindset, revealing the intricate dance between our thoughts, emotions and behaviours. This aspect of personal finance has always fascinated me, especially as I interact with clients, particularly women, and observe their unique attitudes and behaviours towards money.

Central to this exploration is the concept of the money script. Our money script comprises the messages we have internalised about money throughout our lives and the self-talk we engage in daily. These scripts are often subconscious yet significantly influence our financial decisions and overall financial health.

Let me share some fascinating instances of our psychological ties to money that I've encountered. Identify the ones that resonate with you. Once you recognise the factors that influence your behaviour and relationship with money, you'll be better positioned to understand how to approach it and what areas may need improvement.

From a young age, we are exposed to various messages about money from our families, friends and society. These messages can be explicit, such as parents discussing the importance of saving, or implicit, like observing a family member's spending habits. These early experiences form the foundation of our money beliefs and attitudes.

For example, if you frequently heard statements like 'Money doesn't grow on trees' or 'We can't afford that', you might develop a mindset of scarcity and fear around finances. Conversely, if you grew up in an environment where money was freely spent and rarely discussed, you might struggle with budgeting and saving as an adult.

In addition to such external messages, our internal dialogue plays a crucial role in shaping our financial behaviour. Self-talk refers to the thoughts and beliefs we repeat to ourselves about money. These thoughts can be empowering or limiting, depending on the nature of the script.

Consider these two examples of self-talk:

Empowering: 'I am capable of managing my finances and making smart investment decisions.'

Limiting: 'I will never be good with money, and I always make poor financial choices.'

The difference in these scripts can significantly impact your financial decisions and overall financial well-being. Positive self-talk can motivate you to take control of your finances, seek knowledge and make informed choices. Negative self-talk, on the other hand, can lead to avoidance, anxiety and poor financial habits.

To better understand and improve your relationship with money, identify your money script. Here are a few steps to help you uncover and analyse your financial beliefs.

Reflect on your past: Think back to your childhood and early experiences with money. What messages did you receive from your parents, teachers or peers? How did these messages make you feel?

Observe your self-talk: Pay attention to the thoughts you have about money on a daily basis. Are they generally positive or negative? How do they influence your financial behaviour?

Identify patterns: Look for recurring themes or patterns in your money beliefs. Do you notice a tendency towards scarcity, fear or avoidance? Or do you have a strong sense of abundance and confidence?

Challenge negative beliefs: Once you have identified limiting beliefs, challenge them with evidence and positive affirmations. Replace negative self-talk with empowering statements that reflect your financial goals and capabilities.

Seek professional guidance: If you find it challenging to identify or change your money script, consider seeking help from a financial therapist or counselor. They can provide valuable insights and strategies to help you develop a healthier relationship with money.

Understanding your money script is a crucial step towards achieving financial well-being. By recognising the messages you have internalised and the self-talk you engage in, you can begin to reshape your financial mindset. Embrace positive beliefs and affirmations and empower yourself to make informed and confident financial decisions. Remember, your financial future is not solely determined by your past experiences but by the choices you make today.

Let me share some fascinating instances of our psychological ties to money that I've encountered, which will help shed light on the significance of this aspect. Identify which resonates with you. Once you recognize the factors that influence your behaviour and relationship with money, you'll be better positioned to understand how to approach it and what areas may need improvement.

Emotional Attachment to Money

Sneha[4] is a woman who grew up in a frugal household where money was tightly associated with security. From a young age, Sneha witnessed her parents carefully budgeting and saving every rupee, instilling in her the belief that financial stability equated to emotional security. As she grew up, this upbringing deeply influenced Sneha's relationship with money.

---

4 All names have been changed to protect identities.

Now, as an adult, Sneha finds solace in accumulating savings, linking her emotional well-being directly to the size of her bank balance. Whenever she feels stressed or anxious, she turns to her savings as a source of comfort and security, knowing that she has a financial safety net to fall back on. Sneha's attachment to money goes beyond its practical utility; it serves as a tangible symbol of stability and control in her life.

However, while Sneha's inclination towards saving may seem prudent, it's essential for her to understand the underlying emotions driving her financial decisions. By recognising the emotional attachment she has to money, Sneha can navigate her financial journey consciously, ensuring that her saving habits align with her long-term goals and values. She can explore healthier ways to manage her emotions and seek fulfilment beyond the confines of her bank account, ultimately achieving a more balanced and holistic approach to her finances.

Impulse Buying and Instant Gratification

Sarita is a single woman with a stable income who loves browsing online sales for the latest deals and discounts. Sarita often finds herself succumbing to the allure of impulse buying. The convenience of online shopping coupled with enticing discounts makes it challenging for her to resist the temptation of making spontaneous purchases.

Each time Sarita makes an impulse buy, she experiences a momentary rush of excitement and satisfaction. However, this joy is short-lived, and soon remorse sets in as she realises the implications of her impulsive spending. As the novelty of her purchase wears off, Sarita is left grappling with feelings of guilt and regret, wondering if she made the right decision.

It's essential for Sarita to recognise the underlying factors driving her impulse buying behaviour. Perhaps she uses shopping as a way to cope with stress or seek temporary happiness. Understanding the allure of instant gratification and its consequences is crucial for Sarita to break free from this cycle of impulsive spending.

By cultivating self-awareness and practising mindfulness, Sarita can learn to pause and reflect before making a purchase. She can set clear financial goals and establish a budget to guide her spending decisions, prioritising long-term financial satisfaction over momentary gratification. Sarita can also explore healthier outlets for managing stress and finding fulfilment, such as hobbies or spending quality time with loved ones.

Empowered with this understanding, Sarita can take proactive steps to curb her impulsive spending habits and cultivate a more mindful approach to managing her finances. By embracing conscious consumption and practising restraint, Sarita can achieve greater financial stability and ultimately enhance her overall well-being.

Fear of Scarcity

Meet Nisha, who was deeply influenced by her parents' fear of scarcity during her childhood. Growing up, she witnessed her parents constantly worrying about making ends meet, scrimping and saving every penny out of fear of not having enough. This environment instilled in Nisha a deep-seated aversion to financial risk and a pervasive fear of scarcity that lingered into adulthood.

Now as an adult, Nisha's fear of scarcity manifests in her reluctance to take any financial risks, even when presented with promising investment opportunities that align with her goals. Despite understanding the potential for growth and wealth accumulation through investing, Nisha's fear holds her back, causing her to remain stagnant in her financial journey.

Overcoming this fear requires Nisha to delve into its origins and understand how it shapes her beliefs and behaviours around money. By acknowledging the influence of her upbringing and the deep-seated fears instilled by her parents, Nisha can begin to challenge her mindset and approach financial decisions with more confidence and clarity.

Through introspection and financial education, Nisha can gradually overcome her fear of risk and associated scarcity and embrace a more balanced approach to financial management. By recognising that scarcity is not her inevitable fate, Nisha can make informed and confident investment decisions that propel her towards financial security and abundance.

Social Comparisons and Lifestyle Inflation

Ritu finds herself constantly influenced by societal expectations and comparisons with others. Growing up, Ritu was surrounded by a culture that placed great emphasis on outward appearances and material possessions. From the latest fashion trends to extravagant vacations, Ritu felt the pressure to 'keep up' with her peers and maintain a certain standard of living.

As a result, Ritu often finds herself succumbing to the allure of lifestyle inflation, where she increases her spending to match or surpass the perceived lifestyles of those around her. Whether it's upgrading to a bigger house, purchasing luxury items or dining at expensive restaurants, Ritu's financial decisions are heavily influenced by her desire to meet societal expectations and maintain a certain image.

However, the joy she experiences from these fleeting indulgences is short-lived, quickly overshadowed by feelings of guilt and financial strain. Despite her efforts to keep pace with others, she finds herself trapped in a cycle of comparison and dissatisfaction, never feeling truly fulfilled or content with her financial situation.

Understanding the psychological impact of social comparisons is the first step towards breaking free. By recognising that her worth is not defined by external possessions or societal standards, Ritu can begin to redefine her financial goals based on her personal values and priorities.

Through introspection and self-awareness, Ritu can identify what truly brings her fulfilment and happiness, independent of external influences. By shifting her focus from keeping up with others to aligning her financial decisions with her own values and goals, Ritu can regain control over her finances and cultivate a sense of contentment and peace of mind.

Money as a Source of Control

Jasmine is someone who has experienced financial instability in her past. Growing up in a family struggling to make ends meet, Jasmine witnessed firsthand the stress and uncertainty that come with financial hardship. This upbringing instilled in her a deep-seated fear of scarcity and a strong desire for control over her financial circumstances.

As a result, Jasmine views money not just as a means of financial security, but as a source of control over her life. She hoards savings, fearing a return to the scarcity she experienced in her childhood. Every rupee saved represents a sense of control and protection against the unpredictability of the future.

However, Jasmine's quest for control comes at a cost. Her excessive saving habits leave her hesitant to spend on anything beyond the bare essentials, causing her to miss out on opportunities for enjoyment and fulfilment in the present. Despite having the means to afford certain luxuries or experiences, Jasmine's fear of relinquishing control holds her back from fully embracing life's pleasures.

Recognising this need for control is the first step towards finding balance in Jasmine's financial life. By acknowledging the underlying emotions driving her saving habits, Jasmine can begin to strike a healthier balance between planning for the future and enjoying the present. She can explore ways to allocate her savings towards experiences and investments that bring her joy and fulfilment, without compromising her sense of security.

Through mindful spending and financial planning, Jasmine can gradually release the grip of fear and control that has governed her relationship with money. By embracing a more balanced approach to saving and spending, Jasmine can reclaim her financial freedom and cultivate a sense of peace and security that extends beyond her bank account.

Guilt and Financial Decision-Making

Finally, meet Shruti, who was raised in a culture where discussions about money were often considered taboo, particularly for women. From a young age, Shruti internalised the belief that financial matters were best left to men, and that women who took charge of their finances were somehow going against societal norms.

As a result, Shruti feels guilty about making independent financial decisions. Despite having the capability and desire to manage her own money, she hesitates to assert herself in financial matters, fearing judgement or disapproval from others. This guilt weighs heavily on Shruti's shoulders, hindering her ability to take control of her financial destiny.

However, acknowledging this guilt is the first step towards empowerment for Shruti. By recognising the influence of societal norms and cultural expectations on her mindset, Shruti can begin to challenge these ingrained beliefs and assert her right to financial autonomy.

Through open and honest conversations about money with her partner, Shruti can break down the barriers that have long prevented her from taking charge of her financial future. Through a supportive and collaborative environment, Shruti can gain the confidence and support she needs to make informed financial decisions that align with her goals and values.

Overcoming feelings of guilt is a journey, but with each step forward, Shruti becomes more empowered to assert herself in financial matters and shape her own destiny. By embracing her ability to make independent financial decisions, she paves the way for a future of financial freedom and empowerment.

———•———

Understanding these psychological intricacies allows individuals to reshape their relationship with money. It's not merely about budgets and investments; it's about untangling the emotional knots tied to financial decisions. As women embark on the journey of financial empowerment, unravelling these threads becomes instrumental in fostering a healthy and conscious approach to money.

In the vast spectrum of financial behaviours, some women find solace in the act of spending, indulging in retail therapy, while others navigate the path of savers, diligently investing in their future. Yet, both extremes pose risks—financial instability for the spender and missing life's joys for the saver.

The above instances serve as a compass, guiding us to find the optimum balance—where saving and spending converge, leading us on the path to financial freedom. It urges us to be mindful, fostering conscious spending that transcends impulse buying, promising not just financial stability but also a life infused with joy and happiness.

CHAPTER 3

Challenges Faced by Women

'A woman is like a tea bag; you never know how strong it is until it's in hot water.'

—Eleanor Roosevelt

ONCE YOU ARE AWARE OF YOUR PURPOSE AND YOUR RELATIONSHIP WITH money, the next step is to address the challenges you face as a woman. Once you have this clarity, you are better equipped to direct all your energy and resources in the right direction to help keep you focused on achieving your goal.

So are there different rules for women when it comes to personal finance and money management? No, but there are certain unique challenges that women face throughout their financial lives. Being aware of those challenges can help you plan and create effective strategies for reaching your financial goals.

Most of us face this obstacle—the unknown factor that comes in the way of making the right choices with our money. It may be a fear of the unknown for some, while some don't know how much they don't know. Some may feel it is too late to take charge and are embarrassed to ask for help, fearing that their ignorance may come to light.

In this chapter, we explore the distinct wiring of women, their unique approach to money and the challenges they face in taking charge of their financial destinies.

Women's financial compass often points towards holistic well-being, prioritising the security and stability of their families over the mere accumulation of wealth, which often characterises a man's approach. They're less concerned with numerical balances and more focused on ensuring there is food on the table and the future of their children is secured.

This tendency has historical roots. Women have been cast as the caretakers of household finances, fostering a deep understanding of budgeting and long-term planning in them. While men traditionally handled financial affairs, women adeptly managed the family's financial health, prioritising stability amidst societal shifts and economic uncertainties.

Research reveals that women approach financial decisions with a nuanced perspective, weighing risks cautiously and considering a broader spectrum of factors than men typically would.[5] Their inclination towards holistic financial planning underscores their ability to manage both immediate needs and long-term sustainability. This balance is essential to a holistic approach to finances.

Yet, despite their adeptness at managing household finances, women often encounter barriers in asserting their financial power. Societal expectations and subtle biases can erode their

---

5 'Understanding the Female Economy: The Role of Gender in Financial Decision Making and Succession Planning for the Next Generation', *Barclays Wealth*, https://www.findevgateway.org/sites/default/files/publications/files/barclays.pdf.

confidence, leading to feelings of inadequacy or guilt. Many hesitate to seize control of their financial futures, relinquishing decision-making to spouses or partners instead of learning from their mistakes.

Empowering women to recognise and embrace their financial worth is paramount. Tailored financial education and support can equip them with the confidence and skills needed to independently navigate the economic landscape. Addressing the root causes of financial guilt and instilling a sense of empowerment allows them to make informed decisions aligned with their values and goals, unlocking their potential.

Acknowledging and accommodating the unique needs and tendencies of women in financial education and services is crucial. Approaches emphasising collaboration with their spouse, holistic goal setting that takes into account both long-term and short-term needs and risk-aware investment strategies can bridge the gender gap in financial literacy and inclusion, ensuring women's diverse financial needs are met.

Women's financial journey is a tapestry woven with societal, historical and cognitive threads. Empowering them to overcome barriers and make informed decisions is not just a matter of equality but essential for fostering financial well-being for all. By seeking targeted support, recognising their strengths and adopting an inclusive approach to financial education women can confidently navigate the financial landscape and secure a prosperous future for themselves and their families, just as Ritu learnt to do, as we see below.

Sneha Varma belongs to a business family. She lost her husband, who was in his early forties, to an unfortunate accident. They had two children aged eight and twelve, and her old and ailing mother-in-law, who was dependent on them. The premature death of Mr Varma left Sneha in an unbelievably bad state. She had no clue about the family finances and only managed the house expenses with the money her husband would give her at the beginning of the month.

Sneha was in a vulnerable position and had no clue what to do, where to start and whom to trust. A lack of financial literacy would have led her to make some very costly mistakes during those times of grief that could result in her family losing all their money and ending in poverty.

Their family friend's wife, who was an insurance advisor, and their current bank relationship manager (RM), who had been dealing with her husband earlier, had recommended some risky investments. Faced with all these financial decisions, with everyone giving her different advice, Sneha was confused and overwhelmed. Luckily, she was referred to me by her friend for a second opinion, and I was surprised by the recommendations shared by them and their understanding of her needs.

Sensing the situation she and her dependents were in, I decided to handhold her through these decisions. But instead of giving advice that she could blindly follow, I urged her to spend some time understanding money and getting coached so that she no longer needed to depend on anyone and be a victim of her ignorance.

We had to go through a couple of detailed one-on-one coaching sessions to help her come up to speed and know her current situation. She also had to take some tough decisions regarding her future goals and the way forward so that she could sustain the same lifestyle and invest in herself too for the betterment of her future and that of her family.

Today Sneha is financially smart and independent and has ensured her children are financially empowered too.

I get this and I understand that as a woman, you are feeling pulled from all directions. Your children need their mother's undivided attention, your spouse needs your love, your parents and in-laws need your help and support, your career needs your energy and your friends need your time too. Adding to this are household chores, groceries, cleaning, cooking, and it's no surprise that anything to do with money takes the back seat.

But you need to remember this golden rule that is a part of any safety drill—secure yourself first, and then you will be in a much better position to help others.

The right time to enhance your knowledge and get financially empowered is today.

Importance of Financial Literacy for Women

'Education is the most powerful weapon which you can use to change the world.'

—Nelson Mandela

First, what is financial literacy?

Financial literacy encompasses the knowledge and skills required to manage personal finances effectively. It involves understanding various financial concepts, such as budgeting, saving, investing, debt management, insurance and retirement planning.

Financial literacy empowers individuals to make informed decisions about their money and achieve financial stability and independence.

I firmly believe this: 'Financial literacy is financial self-defence.'

Financial self-defence involves being aware, informed and alert, ensuring you're not vulnerable in unforeseen situations. It means being ready to face all the lemons that life throws at you so that you can handle every situation as and when it appears.

And this can be achieved by not just being literate but ... financially literate.

Once you are financially literate, the next step is to be financially smart by applying the knowledge that you have gained, which means having the ability to not let money—or the lack of it—get in the way of your happiness, so that you can make smart and informed life choices. It is being well-equipped with the required knowledge and the tools that are needed to make smart financial decisions.

The Importance of Asking Questions

Ladies, when it comes to your finances, never hesitate to ask questions. Understanding is key to making informed decisions. One of my clients, a gynaecologist, once shared a frustrating experience. During meetings with bank relationship managers, terms like PMS were casually thrown around. For her, PMS meant Pre-Menstrual Syndrome, not Portfolio Management Services. The RM assumed she was familiar with financial jargon, often directing the conversation towards her husband and alienating her, despite her being the one interested in investing. This situation isn't uncommon. Many financial advisors use terms like YTM, PMS and IRR, which can be daunting if you're not from a finance background. It's okay to ask for clarification. Your financial future matters and being informed empowers you to take charge. Don't let unfamiliar terms or assumptions hold you back. Ask questions, seek clarity and build your financial confidence. Together, let's bridge the knowledge gap and empower ourselves in the world of finance.

She shut off and deferred her decision to invest, feeling alienated by the financial jargon and assumptions made during those meetings. In the end, who really lost out? We got introduced after two years, and she confided in me about her experience. She had deferred investing her money then, feeling put off by the previous advisor's approach. It was only after she felt heard and understood that she chose to invest. This incident made me reflect deeply. The previous advisor should have recognised her discomfort and clarified terms, fostering a trusting relationship. Instead, assumptions and miscommunication led to missed opportunities. In the end, it was both the advisor and the client who lost out on potential gains. Effective communication and understanding are crucial in financial advising, ensuring clients feel respected and empowered in their financial decisions.

Financial literacy is indispensable for all individuals, irrespective of gender. Yet, its importance needs to be especially emphasised for women, who are more easily influenced by diverse societal and economic dynamics. Taking ownership of your life empowers you to better support your loved ones.

My earnest request to you is this: Prioritise for yourself as you do for others. Remember, self-investment isn't selfish; it's essential for holistic well-being.

You don't need to be 'exceptional with numbers' or an expert with complex calculations to master your money. You just need to be aware and alert and develop some good healthy habits and have the right attitude to be financially smart. Yes, you have it in you.

Here are some simple yet crucial things that women should remember regarding financial literacy:

BE FINANCIALLY SMART

1. *Don't hesitate to ask for clarifications*: If you don't understand something related to finances, don't feel shy or intimidated to ask questions. It's essential to have a clear understanding to make informed decisions.

2. *Make financial management a family affair*: Engage your family members in discussions about financial goals, budgeting and planning. Creating a supportive environment where everyone is involved can lead to better financial outcomes. It could be as simple as buying a mobile, a TV or going on a pilgrimage or a vacation with family.

3. *Stay aware and involved*: Even if someone else manages the household finances, stay informed and involved in them. We are not talking here of only updating the passbook, filing papers or signing a cheque. These are everyday tasks already handled by most women. Being aware of cash flows, bill payments and investments ensures financial stability and reduces vulnerabilities by helping to plug unnecessary and avoidable financial leakages.

4. *Learn basic financial skills*: Understand how to operate a bank account, manage cash flows and effectively utilise financial products and services.

5. *Understand key financial concepts*: Familiarise yourself with concepts like inflation, the compounding effect of money and the importance of risk management—life and health. Having a grasp of these concepts will help you make sound financial decisions.

6. *Protect yourself and your loved ones*: Ensure you have adequate insurance coverage for life, health and property. Review policies regularly and ensure nominations are up to date.

7. *Explore investment options*: Understand different investment vehicles and consider aligning investments with your values and goals. Be aware of the difference between insurance and investment.

8. *Be proactive*: Take charge of your financial life by setting SMART goals (as we will discuss later). Regularly review your progress and make adjustments as needed. Check if your values are aligned with your goals.

9. *Stay vigilant against fraud*: Be aware of common financial scams and take steps to protect yourself and your personal information.

10. *Practise self-care*: Remember that managing finances is not just about numbers; it's also about your well-being. Take care of yourself physically, emotionally and financially to lead a balanced and fulfilling life.

By keeping these simple yet effective tips in mind, women can enhance their financial literacy and confidently navigate their financial journey.

Once you are well informed about your financial life, the available options and what to expect from it, you will be in a much better position to take a calculated risk that can help you make smart and informed choices to enable you to reach your goal faster. This will surely boost your confidence.

Knowledge that is acquired and stored and not put into relevant action has seldom helped anyone.

Being prepared will help each one of us manage things seamlessly in case of the occurrence of any unfortunate event, whether it's the loss of a loved one or a financial loss, or whether it is feeling empowered about the money you have gained and knowing what you're going to do with it.

It's time to take back control of your financial life! And I am proud of you … as you have taken this crucial step.

With this premise, let us step deeper to learn and understand some important concepts and the S.M.A.R.T.E.R way to wealth that every financially smart and empowered woman needs to know.

It's Time to Rise and Get Financially Smart

'The only way to deal with the future is to function efficiently in the now.'

—Gita Bellin

Dear sister, hear me out today.
For your financial life, it's time to slay.
Don't wait for fate to take the lead!
It's time to step up and take the lead.

You're awesome at most things, we know.
Saving and managing expenses, you've got the flow.
But it's time to focus on assets that can grow
And make informed decisions as you go.

Don't let others control your fate.
Your finances are yours to create.

BE FINANCIALLY SMART

You're an entrepreneur, a CFO, a success.
But financial independence, you must address.

Don't just live pay check to pay check,
Splurging on luxuries, a financial wreck.
Focus on long-term goals and financial security
And watch your bank account grow, with clarity.

Yes, there are challenges, we know.
Breaks in career, lower pay and more.
But with discipline, knowledge and grit
You can overcome, and never quit.

So sister, it's time to get financially smart.
Make smart decisions, right from the start.
Invest in your education, your future, your life
And say goodbye to financial strife.

Remember, you're not alone in this fight.
We're here to support, to inspire and ignite.
Let's break the stereotypes, the barriers, the norms!
And create a financial future that transforms.

So, let's raise a glass, to you and me
To financial independence, to be free.
Let's take the reins and pave the way!
For a brighter future, starting today!

Section 2

Important Concepts Every Financially Smart and Empowered Woman Needs to Know

As a financially smart and empowered woman, you understand that money plays a critical role in shaping your present and future. You are not content with simply earning and spending money, but you want to make sure that your hard-earned money works for you. But to do that, you need to understand some crucial concepts that can help you navigate the complex world of finance.

In this section of this book, we will explore some of the most important concepts that every woman needs to know. From avoiding costly money mistakes to understanding the power of compounding, from managing your money effectively to understanding the cost of delay, this section will equip you with the knowledge and tools you need to take control of your financial future.

Five Common but Costly Money Mistakes

'Mistakes are the portals of discovery.'

—James Joyce

Welcome to the world of financial empowerment!

Earning money is just the beginning of your journey towards financial independence. The real magic happens when you make your money work for you. However, many women unknowingly make common but costly money mistakes that can eventually have a huge impact on their financial well-being. Knowing what mistakes to avoid is just as important as knowing what actions to take. As the saying goes, you don't have to go through something yourself to learn from it; learning from others' mistakes is also valuable and helps you make smarter decisions.

In this chapter, we will discuss the top five money mistakes that women tend to make and offer practical tips on how to avoid them. By following these simple principles, you can take charge of your financial life and become a Financially Smart

Woman. So, let's dive in and discover the secrets of making your money work for you!

Mistake #1: Not paying yourself first

Saving is essential to achieving your financial goals. One of the smartest financial habits you can develop is paying yourself first. Treat saving like any other expense by regularly setting aside a fixed amount. Automating this process ensures that you are consistent in your savings habit. Think of this as investing in your future and empowering yourself financially.

Mistake #2: Not budgeting

Do you know where all your money goes? Financially empowered women know precisely how much money is coming in and how much is going out. They have a budget that outlines their income, expenses and savings. This helps them be in control of their finances and make informed financial decisions. So, make sure you have a budget and follow it diligently.

Mistake #3: Saving but not investing

Saving is essential, but it is not enough to achieve your long-term financial goals. While savings are safe and easily accessible, investing your money helps it grow and work for you. Even a small investment amount can eventually yield high returns. So, start investing today and watch your money grow.

Mistake #4: Not having an emergency fund

Life is unpredictable, and emergencies can happen at any time. Having an emergency fund of six to nine months' expenses will provide you with financial security in case of job loss, illness or unexpected expenses. Keep this fund in a savings or fixed deposit account that is easily accessible.

Mistake #5: Not having a health and life insurance plan

Risk management is crucial in financial planning. A health insurance plan covers hospitalisation expenses for you and your family members. A term life insurance policy ensures that your family's financial needs are taken care of in case of the sudden death of an earning family member. Make sure you have adequate coverage for yourself and your family.

Exercise

Now that you know about these common mistakes, it's time to assess your financial habits. Answer the following questions to determine where you stand:

1. Do you pay yourself first?
2. Do you have an emergency fund that covers six to nine months of your expenses?
3. Do you invest your money as per your financial goals?
4. Are your investments protected against inflation?
5. Do you have a budget that outlines your income, expenses and savings?
6. Do you have a health insurance policy that covers you and your family members?
7. Do you have adequate term life insurance coverage for yourself and the earning members of your family?

> 8. Do you know how much life insurance cover & health insurance you and your family need?
> 9. Do you have your SMART goals written down?
> 10. Do you know how much is needed to achieve each of your goals, especially your financial freedom goal?

If you answered 'No' or 'Not aware' to any of these questions, don't worry.

By the end of this book, you will be equipped with the knowledge and tools you need to make smart financial decisions and take control of your financial future.

What Is Inflation and How Is It Affecting Your Money?

'Inflation is taxation without legislation.'
—Milton Friedman

HAVE YOU EVER WONDERED IF A RUPEE IS ALWAYS WORTH A RUPEE?

It may seem like a silly question, but the value of a rupee is not always the same. The value of money changes dramatically depending on when you get it and what you do with it. Time plays a crucial role in determining the exact value of your money, and inflation is the silent killer that decreases the spending power of each rupee you have.

For instance, if you keep ₹100 in your money box for a year, you will still have ₹100 at the end of the year. However, due to inflation, ₹100 may buy less than it does now.

Let me tell you the story of my Aunt Reena who loved watching movies. Reena grew up in the 1960s and her favourite movie was *Sholay*. She still remembers the day when she watched the movie for the first time with her father. They went to a small theatre in their neighbourhood.

Years went by, and Reena grew up to be a successful corporate executive. One Sunday, as she and her family were watching the movie *Sholay* at her parents' place, her father and she reminisced the first time they watched it in the theatre years ago. Her father asked her if she was aware what the price of the ticket was then in 1975. She said may be around ₹50 or so. Her father laughed and said the ticket price was just ₹4.50.

Reena was shocked by the stark difference in the ticket price. The price of a ticket in any multiplex today is at least ₹250. This meant that the purchasing power of a rupee had reduced drastically over the years: with just ₹5 now, she wouldn't be able to afford anything. She could not understand how the price could increase so much over the years. This is when she remembered inflation. Her father told her, 'Like the villain in any movie, inflation is the silent killer—the villain in our financial journey. If we ignore it, we need to be ready for a rude shock.' It erodes our money; hence, we need to be aware of this very important concept and plan and invest our money wisely.

So, what is inflation? Inflation is a steady increase in the price of goods and services over time. It means that the value of money decreases over time, and you would need more money to buy the same thing in the future.

Reena realised that the ticket price for a movie had increased by fifty times over the last forty-nine years. This meant that the value of a rupee in 1975 was different from the value of a rupee in 2024.

Reena needed to be aware of inflation and its effects on her money. Inflation was a natural part of the economy, and she needed to take steps to protect her money from its effects. She started to invest her money in ways that would protect her from inflation, such as investing in mutual funds and other asset classes.

Inflation is a crucial economic concept because it affects the purchasing power of our money over time. When prices rise, the same amount of money buys fewer goods and services. This means that if we don't account for inflation, our savings and income can lose value, making it harder to afford the things we need and want.

Inflation is the gradual rise in the prices of goods and services over time, which can have significant long-term effects on our finances. While it may seem insignificant year to year, its cumulative impact can erode our purchasing power.

Unmasking the Effects of Inflation

Inflation's influence extends across various facets of our lives, often subtly. To understand its impact, let us explore several critical domains in which the impact of inflation is drastic:

Food Inflation

Let's understand this with the help of an example of a popular butter brand.

Do you still have cosy mornings when you enjoy crispy toast slathered with delicious butter? That was our family's favourite breakfast when I was growing up, a simple joy amidst our busy lives.

Commodity Inflation—The Impact of Oil Prices

Consider ₹100 in 1985. With that amount, you could purchase 12.5 litres of petrol. Fast forward to 2007, and the same ₹100 would only buy you 2 litres of petrol. Today, on 28 March 2024, as I am writing this, petrol is priced at ₹104.21 per litre in Mumbai. That ₹100 will only afford you approximately 0.96 litres of petrol today.

This example illustrates how inflation diminishes the value of money over time. Essentially, while our nominal wealth may remain the same, the real purchasing power of our money decreases. This phenomenon affects not only petrol but all the goods and services we rely on, highlighting the profound impact of inflation on our everyday lives.

Medical Inflation

Let me introduce you to Sonal, a dedicated professional and friend in her mid-forties, whose life took an unexpected turn when she was involved in an accident that led to her hospitalisation. Her journey through the complexities of the healthcare system shed light on the harsh realities of medical inflation.

It all began on a routine day when Sonal was involved in a serious car accident. The impact was severe, and she was rushed to the hospital for immediate medical attention. Sonal underwent a series of tests and procedures to assess the extent of her injuries and determine the necessary course of treatment.

Despite having what she believed to be comprehensive insurance coverage, Sonal was taken aback by the staggering costs of essential medical procedures. The expenses for treatments and interventions had surged significantly over the past five years, placing an unexpected financial burden on her shoulders, as a result of medical inflation. She hadn't realised that her insurance might not cover everything, and it made her wish she had increased her medical cover over the years.

Sonal saw firsthand how hard it was for people to afford healthcare. The COVID-19 pandemic had made things even worse, with more people needing medical help and bills getting even higher. She wasn't sure how she would manage if she needed more treatments in the future.

In the middle of all this, Sonal realised she needed to take action to understand her options better. She started researching how healthcare pricing worked and what her insurance covered. She wanted to be smarter about her healthcare choices and how she managed her money.

Inspired by her own struggles, Sonal decided to speak up for others facing the same challenges. She wanted to see more transparency in healthcare costs and changes to control how much prices were going up. Sonal believed everyone should be able to afford quality healthcare without worrying about money.

Sonal's story reminds us all about how tough it can be to deal with rising healthcare costs. She's determined to make a difference and hopes to start conversations about making healthcare more affordable for everyone.

STUNNING SPIKE Medical costs have zoomed in 5 years

Procedures	2012	2007	Increase
Childbirth (Caesarean)	42,000	29,000	45%
Childbirth (Normal)	26,000	18,000	44%
Cataract Removal	24,000	16,000	50%
Angiography	22,000	14,000	57%
Coronary Artery Bypass Graft (CABG)	2,35,000	1,65,000	42%
Appendectomy	42,000	28,000	50%
Haemorrhoidectomy (Piles)	35,000	21,000	67%
Cholecystectomy (Gall Bladder Removal)	52,000	32,000	63%
TURP (Prostate Surgery)	62,000	37,000	68%
Angioplasty (PTCA) with 2 stents	2,45,000	1,55,000	58%

Source: Medimanage Insurance Broking

Education Inflation

If your child's school tuition was ₹50,000 per year last year, you might expect to pay around ₹55,000 per year this year due to inflation.

Let's understand this with a real case scenario. Imagine you were planning for your son's college education back in 2010. At that time, you researched the cost of attending a reputable university and estimated it to be around ₹10 lakhs for a four-year degree programme.

You were diligently saving and investing towards this goal, as you realised the importance of education in shaping your son's future. However, as the years went by, you became increasingly aware of the effects of inflation on education costs.

Fast forward to 2022, the year your son is set to enter college. Upon revisiting the cost of education, you were shocked to find out that the same four-year degree programme that was estimated at ₹10 lakhs in 2010 had gone up significantly. Due to the rising costs of tuition, accommodation and other expenses, the total cost for the same programme had now escalated to around ₹20 lakhs.

This scenario vividly illustrates the impact of inflation on long-term financial planning for education. Despite your initial estimates and savings, the actual cost of your son's education doubled over the span of twelve years due to inflation.

This example emphasises the necessity of incorporating inflation projections into your financial planning. It underscores the importance of regularly reassessing your savings goals and investment strategies to ensure they keep pace with the rising costs of education, safeguarding your ability to provide the best opportunities for your child's future. Ignoring educational inflation can lead to unexpected financial burdens and hinder the achievement of educational aspirations.

Overall, inflation is an important concept to understand because it affects the value of the money we earn and save. To become a financially empowered woman, you must include inflation in all your calculations and projections so that you aren't caught off-guard at the eroding value of your hard-earned money.

CHAPTER 3

Empowering Women Through the Time Value of Money

'Time is money.'

—Benjamin Franklin

As an Indian woman navigating the dynamic landscape of personal finance, understanding the time value of money (TVM) becomes paramount. This financial concept, encapsulating the intricate interplay between time, money and interest rates, serves as a guiding light for making judicious decisions across diverse financial goals, whether it's securing your child's education, planning for retirement or undertaking entrepreneurial endeavours.

Reflecting on my own journey, which commenced in the economic landscape of the 1990s, I see the twists and turns that have defined my financial path. From earning a modest ₹3000 per month at the age of nineteen to witnessing market

48

upheavals like the Harshad Mehta scam in 1992, my journey echoes the unpredictable nature of both life and finance.

In those early years, when the BSE Sensex soared to an all-time high of 4,630.54 points in 1994, the financial realm appeared mysterious and distant. Fixed deposits, traditional insurance and post office schemes provided solace in a seemingly complex world. Little did we realise that understanding and engaging with instruments like the Sensex could be instrumental in our financial voyage.

The 1990s boasted fixed deposit interest rates of around 13%, a far cry from the present scenario. If only I had ventured into investing ₹1,000 per month back then—today's narrative might have been vastly different. Lack of knowledge, fear of markets and a dearth of financial literacy were formidable barriers that hindered many from exploring these opportunities.

Fast forward to June 2024, and the Sensex is approaching the pinnacle of ₹77,000. The financial landscape has evolved, demanding a corresponding evolution in our financial strategies. As women, it's time we seize control of our financial destinies, shattering the barriers of fear, misinformation and the misconception that finance is not our domain.

Effect of Getting an Early Start

In a small town in India, there lived two college friends of the same age, Radhika and Neha. Both were smart and ambitious women, keen on securing their financial futures. They understood the importance of saving and investing, but their approaches were quite different.

Radhika, always a forward-thinker, decided to start investing at the age of twenty-five. She committed to putting away

₹10,000 every month into an investment plan that offered a 12% annual return. She planned to keep this up for twenty years.

Every month, she diligently invested ₹10,000. By the end of the twenty-year period, she had invested a total of ₹24,00,000. Thanks to the power of compounding, her investment grew substantially over time. By the time she turned forty-five, her investment had blossomed into a substantial ₹99,91,480.

Neha, on the other hand, didn't start investing until she was thirty. She however decided to invest ₹15,000 every month in the same 12% annual return plan, thinking she will catch up for the lost time. She planned to do this for fifteen years.

After investing ₹15,000 each month for fifteen years, Neha had invested a total of ₹27,00,000 by the time she turned forty-five. However, her investment had grown only to ₹75,68,640.

Investment Comparison Table

Investor	Monthly Investment (₹)	Investment Period (Years)	Total Investment (₹)	Final Value (₹)
Radhika	10,000	20	24,00,000	99,91,480
Neha	15,000	15	27,00,000	75,68,640

The Lesson of Time

So why was there a difference in the amount of money they ended up with? The answer lies in the time value of money (TVM). This financial concept tells us that money available today is worth more than the same amount in the future because of its potential to grow.

Radhika's early start allowed her money to grow and compound for a longer period. Compounding is like a snowball effect—each year, the interest earned gets added to the principal, and the interest for the next year is calculated on this larger amount. This means the longer you invest, the more your money can grow.

Neha, although investing a larger amount each month, had less time for her money to grow and compound. Starting five years later meant she missed crucial years of growth and compounding, which made a significant difference in her final amount.

This story of Radhika and Neha highlights the importance of starting early when it comes to investing. Whether you are saving for your child's education, planning for retirement or thinking about starting a business, remember the lesson from their journey. Start investing as early as you can to give your money the best chance to grow.

By understanding and applying the time value of money, you can make more informed and beneficial financial decisions, ensuring a brighter and more secure future.

Despite investing a larger amount each month, Neha's final amount (corpus accumulated) was lower than Radhika's due to the shorter compounding period.

This comparison highlights the importance of starting early. Even with a lower monthly investment, starting sooner allowed Radhika's investment to grow significantly more than Neha's. This demonstrates the transformative influence of the time value of money and the power of compounding over time.

Investing money early can significantly boost your earnings potential. When interest rates are higher, your financial growth accelerates even more. Time plays a crucial role here too: *the sooner you start investing, the more time your money has to grow.*

Starting your investment journey early, even with a small amount, sets a solid foundation. Each rupee you invest starts earning interest, which compounds over time. This compounding effect can rapidly accelerate your progress towards financial goals.

Understanding the time value of money and the power of compounding is essential for Indian women making smart financial decisions. Starting investments early is key because time is your greatest ally in achieving financial success.

As you grasp these concepts, consider passing this wisdom on to the next generation. Teach your teenage children and young adults about the importance of saving and investing early. By engaging them in discussions about money, you're helping to shape their financial futures. They'll thank you one day for starting them on the path to financial security.

Now, let's check the impact of a cost delay of just one year.

Two friends named Sita and Gita decided to start investing ₹20,000 per month to secure their future financial stability. However, Sita decided to start investing at the age of twenty-five, while Gita thought she would wait for a year and start at age twenty-six. Gita believed that delaying her investment by one year wouldn't make much of a difference, as she was due for a salary increase and one of her policy pay-outs was also due next year.

Years went by, and they both continued investing. At the age of forty, Sita's total investment had grown to a staggering ₹1 crore, while Gita's investment was only ₹87 lakhs. That is a difference of ₹13 lakhs!

How did this happen? Here again, the answer lies in the power of compounding. The longer you invest, the more your investment earns through interest or returns, which are reinvested, leading to a snowball effect over time. Even a small delay in starting to invest can cost you a lot of money eventually.

Investor	Monthly Investment (₹)	Investment Period (Years)	Final Amount at 12% Annual Return
Sita	20,000	15	1 crore
Gita	20,000	14	87 lakhs
Difference	-	-	13.63 lakhs

The last row indicates the difference in the final amount between Sita and Gita, which is ₹13.63 lakhs. Despite starting just one year later and investing ₹2.4 lakhs less, Gita's final amount was ₹13.63 lakhs less than Sita's due to the compounding effect over time.

This table succinctly illustrates the financial impact of delaying investments by just one year, emphasising the importance of starting early to maximise returns through compounding.

So, if you have not started investing yet, start today. Don't wait for the 'right time' or a 'better opportunity' because time is the one thing that you can't get back. The cost of delay can be high, and it is never too early or too late to start investing in your future.

You can try out this calculation for yourself by visiting our website and checking out the calculators: https://www.moneyprastha.com/Calculators.html.

The Magical Power of Compounding

'The most powerful force in the universe is compound interest.'
—Albert Einstein

LET US NOW LOOK MORE CLOSELY AT A COMPLEMENTARY CONCEPT: THE magical power of compounding and how it can help you achieve your financial goals. Compounding refers to the process of earning interest on your interest, which can result in the exponential growth of your savings or investments over time. Long ago, there was an Indian king who was very fond of playing chess. He was proud of his skill and would always play friendly matches with the scholars in his court. Whenever a new traveller entered his kingdom, he would challenge them to a game of chess. If they beat him, he would reward them with any treasure or prize they desired.

One day, a pilgrim wandered into his kingdom and was challenged to a game by the king. What the king did not know was that the pilgrim was a mathematician and a chess expert. The pilgrim won the game, and the crowd was shocked. The king kept his promise and told him, 'Ask for whatever you want.'

The mathematician was a smart person. He said, 'Your Highness, my wish is very simple. All I ask for is one grain of rice for the first square of the chessboard and then double the grain of rice for every following square.'

The king laughed. He thought the mathematician was foolish. He could ask for anything, gold, land or even a part of his kingdom, but he wanted only a few grains of rice. The king gave the command, and his servants began placing grains of rice upon the chessboard—one in the first square and two in the second.

For the third square, the emperor gave 4, then 8, followed by 16, 32, 64 and 128. On the fourteenth square, the emperor had to give 2048 grains of rice. Things became interesting after twenty-eight squares, when the weight of the grains had crossed almost 1,000 tonnes. By the thirtieth square, the king had to put down 1 billion grains of rice.

He did not need to reach the 64th and final square as he would need to reward the pilgrim with roughly 18,000,000,000,000,000,000 (that's eighteen million trillion) grains of rice, which is more rice than the entire nation of India could imagine.

Obviously, the king could not pay and was declared bankrupt. The mathematician then took over the empire and lived happily ever after.

This story illustrates the power of compounding, where a small amount of rice grains on the first square grows exponentially to a massive amount on the last square of the chessboard. The same concept applies to your savings or investments. A small amount of money invested regularly can grow exponentially over time. Compounding can make a significant difference in whether and when you achieve your financial goals.

Let's apply this to real money. Let's understand it with the example of Renuka, who started investing ₹5,000 per month in a mutual fund at the age of 25. Assuming a 12% annual rate of return, she would have invested a total of ₹12 lakhs over 20 years, and her investment would have grown to around ₹50 lakhs thanks to compounding.

> **Power of SIP Calculator**—Use this calculator to see how small investments made at regular intervals (SIPs) can grow to a large figure over a period of time with power of compounding.
>
> https://www.moneyprastha.com/Calculators.html

By starting early and investing regularly, Renuka was able to take advantage of the power of compounding and grow her investment exponentially over time. The key takeaway from Renuka's example is that the longer you stay invested, the more time your money has to grow and compound.

Goal SIP Calculator

> Plan for your goals by using this calculator to determine the monthly SIP investments you need to make to reach a particular goal.
>
> https://www.moneyprastha.com/Calculators.html

Let's also check some calculations in case of *lump sum deposit* and the benefits of the power of compounding:

Time	Value of ₹50,00,000 at 8% pa interest
After 5 years	₹73,46,640
After 10 years	₹1,07,94,625
After 15 years	₹1,58,60,846
After 20 years	₹2,33,04,786
After 25 years	₹3,42,42,376
After 30 years	₹5,03,13,284
After 35 years	₹7,39,26,721

In conclusion, the power of compounding is a magical tool that can help us achieve our financial goals. By starting early and investing regularly, you can take advantage of the power of compounding and grow your savings or investments exponentially over time.

So, start investing today, and let the power of compounding work its magic for you!

Money Management Skills

'A budget is telling your money where to go instead of wondering where it went.'

—Dave Ramsey

MONEY IS A TOOL THAT CAN BE A MEANS TO AN END, BUT IT CAN'T BUY happiness. It's essential to respect and honour your money, and this begins with arranging your wallet and bills. Knowing how to work towards SMART goals is crucial. However, the most critical life skill you need to learn is money management. Unfortunately, schools or colleges don't teach us this skill.

Managing your finances should be a priority, and it should influence your daily spending and saving decisions. It demands constant attention to your spending and accounts and requires the discipline of not living beyond your means. Many people think they will save money when they make more, but even then, they have no idea where it goes.

The Smart Life Account is an effective method that can help you achieve remarkable results. This simple system involves splitting your money into two main accounts and then distributing it into five other accounts or envelopes, as percentages of your money allocated to each account. You can use bank accounts or jars, buckets, boxes or envelopes.

Let's unveil the SMART Money Management Accounting System—a dynamic approach that adapts to your financial goals and lifestyle, whether you're an individual or part of a couple.

> **Smart Tip** - It's important to note that the percentages given below are recommendations and not definitive rules. The habit of managing your money is far more important than the amount. If you can't follow the percentages accurately, start with an amount you can manage, and gradually increase it.

The SMART Money Management Accounting System

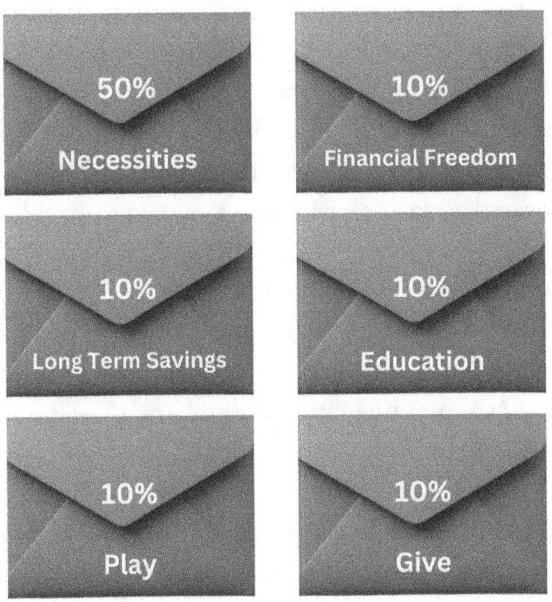

Start by dividing the total amount received from all your income sources into two accounts: the Essentials Account and the Growth Account.

1. *Essentials Account*: Allocate around 50% of the total money here once you check your cashflows. This is your primary spending account, covering necessities like rent, utilities, groceries and transportation. This ensures your essential needs are met without financial stress.

    Smart Tip: *If 55% of your income doesn't cover all your necessities, you need to simplify your life or find ways to earn more.*

2. *Growth Account*: This account pertains to all the money needed for your personal growth and to build a corpus for your various lifetime goals, including the key goal— financial freedom. The balance 50% remaining after parking the amount towards the essentials further needs to be divided into five specialised accounts that can be kept in plastic envelopes initially or separate bank accounts with the relevant name tag. Feel free to use the latest apps available or a simple Excel sheet to bifurcate the amounts. The trick is to ensure you have access only to the money allocated as decided by you.

The five envelopes are as follows:

1) *Freedom Fund Account: 10%.* Reserved for building wealth for your future financial freedom. You should never spend this money.

2) *Long-Term Saving and Spending for Goals Account: 15%.* Dedicated to funding your short- and long-term SMART goals. Invest based on your planned time frame and to be

spent for achieving your set goals. Use this account to save for future expenses, such as a new car, a vacation, a new couch, the down payment for a house, gifts or repaying debts.

3) *Personal Development Account: 10%.* Invest in your personal development and growth. This can include courses, workshops or any form of education that enhances your knowledge, skills and career prospects and can thus increase your earning capacity.

4) *Play Account: 10%.* Intended for personal enjoyment, small luxuries and rewards. Use this for activities that motivate, treat and pamper yourself. This allows you to spend without guilt and gradually improve your standard of living as your income increases.

5) *Giving Account: 5%.* Cultivate the habit of giving without expectation. This amount is reserved for charitable donations or contributions to causes that resonate with you. Giving away part of your income can also help you feel abundance and give you satisfaction.

Let's assume a cumulative monthly income of ₹1,00,000. Using the Smart Six Money Jar Method, here's how the percentages would translate into actual amounts:

Money Jar	Percentage	Amount (₹)
Necessities	50%	₹50,000
Financial Freedom	10%	₹10,000
Long-Term Savings	15%	₹15,000
Education and Growth	10%	₹10,000
Lifestyle	10%	₹10,000
Giving Back	5%	₹5,000

This breakdown ensures a balanced approach to managing finances, covering both immediate needs and future aspirations while also fostering personal growth and social responsibility.

Remember, managing your money is a crucial life skill that requires constant attention and discipline. Use the Smart Life Account method to simplify your finances and achieve your financial goals. Start small and build the habit of managing your money, so you never fall short of funds. Do try this out and share your feedback, queries and experiences.

CHAPTER 6

Empower Your Financial Journey with the S.M.A.R.T.E.R Way to Wealth

'Automate your finances: Pay yourself first and build wealth without thinking about it.'

—David Bach

TOGETHER, LET'S EMBARK ON A TRANSFORMATIVE JOURNEY TOWARDS financial empowerment through the lens of the S.M.A.R.T.E.R Way to Wealth framework. Designed to equip you with practical strategies and invaluable insights, this framework serves as a compass, guiding you through the intricacies of finance and propelling you towards your envisioned financial future.

Let's delve into each element of this awesome framework and unearth its transformative potential for your financial empowerment.

Element 1: S - Savings as a Foundation. Savings form the bedrock of financial security. It's more than routine deposits; it's about cultivating a savings habit. Start by allocating a portion of your income, regardless of the amount. Over time, these contributions accumulate to safeguard you against emergencies and fund future aspirations.

Element 2: M - Mastering Money Management. Money management is your key to informed choices. Develop a comprehensive budget aligned with your goals and values. Monitor cash flows, optimise expenditures and distinguish between needs and wants. Sharpen this skill to maximise resource utilisation.

Follow the SMART Money Management Account System discussed earlier.

Element 3: A - Attitude, Your Financial Mindset. Your financial attitude shapes your reality. Scrutinise beliefs, messages and feelings about money. Shed limiting notions and cultivate a positive outlook. Embrace gratitude for your current situation and envision your financial aspirations with unwavering optimism.

Element 4: R - Resources for Learning and Growth. The financial landscape offers a wealth of resources—books, courses, webinars and more. But resourcefulness matters equally. Vet content for relevance and credibility. Leverage technology judiciously to access valuable insights.

Element 5: T - Time, the Compounding Catalyst. Time is your ally in wealth accumulation. Commence your investment journey early, allowing compounding to work its magic over years. Understand its role as a silent yet powerful contributor to financial growth.

Element 6: E – Equity for Wealth Expansion. Equity investments counter inflation and amplify wealth. Diversify your assets intelligently, allowing your money to work for you. Harness the potential of equity to unlock growth and mitigate the effects of inflation.

Element 7: R – Regular Review for Progress. Consistent evaluation is your compass on this journey. Schedule regular 'money dates' to assess your budget, cash flows, investments and mindset. Check and plug your leakages if any from time to time. Modify strategies, celebrate milestones and ensure alignment with your goals.

The S.M.A.R.T.E.R Way to Wealth is your guide, propelling you through the intricacies of finance. Embrace these principles—Savings, Money Management, Attitude, Resources, Time, Equity, and Regular Review—as pillars of your financial journey.

It's time you are SET out on your journey by following and keeping in mind the three main components from the above framework here to make your money work for you and help you get set on your journey to be financially free:

S - Saving and ensuring you focus on increasing your savings rate annually.

E- Equity can help you generate wealth; so invest in equity.

T- Time is the most important element as we have repeatedly shared. Allow the magical power of compounding to work for you.

Remember, financial mastery is a lifelong pursuit, marked by growth and empowerment. Armed with these principles, you're poised to navigate financial complexities and carve a path to your envisioned financial future.

Action Points

1. Cultivate a consistent savings habit for financial stability.
2. Master the art of money management so as to make informed decisions.
3. Shape a positive financial attitude, shedding limiting beliefs.
4. Utilise resources judiciously to enhance financial wisdom.
5. Recognise the compounding potential of time in your investments.
6. Leverage equity investments to propel wealth expansion.
7. Implement regular reviews through scheduled 'money dates'.
8. Embark on your lifelong journey towards financial empowerment with determination.

Section 3

Your Financially SMART Blueprint

Congratulations! You have made it to the third section of this book!

By now, you have gained valuable knowledge on the most critical concepts that every financially empowered woman should know. However, it is time to act and create a blueprint for your financial success.

In this section, we will guide you through creating your Financially SMART Blueprint, a comprehensive financial plan that will set you up for success. From opening a bank account and creating a SMART budget plan to protecting your family and home, we will cover all aspects of financial planning.

It's time to take control of your financial future and design a plan that works for you. Let's redefine life planning for a fulfilling future.

The Intersection of Life Planning and Financial Planning

'Planning is bringing the future into the present so that you can do something about it now.'

—Alan Lakein

IN TODAY'S WORLD, FINANCIAL PLANNING HAS BECOME AN INTEGRAL part of our lives. But for women, it is essential to realise that traditional financial planning methods do not always work. Instead, a more comprehensive approach that combines life planning and financial planning is required to achieve financial independence and a fulfilling future.

This chapter delves into the world of life planning and its intersection with financial planning. We explore real-life stories of women from all walks of life who have achieved financial freedom by redefining their goals and reimagining their lives.

Life Planning and Its Importance

Financial Life planning is not merely about numbers on a spreadsheet; it's about discovering your true self, your values and your aspirations. In this section, we explore the transformative power of life planning through the inspiring journey of Maya, a successful corporate executive who dared to embark on a path of self-discovery and fulfilment.

Maya appeared to have it all—a prestigious career, financial stability and societal recognition. Yet, behind the façade of success, she grappled with a profound sense of disillusionment and unfulfillment. Despite her outward achievements, Maya felt adrift, lacking a deeper sense of purpose and meaning in her life.

When Maya dedicated some time to life planning, Maya realised that there was more to life than her corporate career and material success. Through introspection and self-exploration, she unearthed her long-suppressed desire to make a meaningful impact on others' lives. Maya's story underscores the importance of adopting a holistic approach to planning that acknowledges the intrinsic connection between personal fulfilment and financial well-being.

Empowered by newfound clarity, Maya made the bold decision to pursue her passion for social entrepreneurship. Despite the inherent risks and uncertainties, she embraced the opportunity to align her professional endeavours with her core values and aspirations.

As she embarked on her entrepreneurial journey, she encountered numerous challenges and setbacks. Yet, amidst the struggles, she found fulfilment in knowing that every endeavour was a step towards realising her vision of creating positive change in the world.

Through life planning, Maya not only reclaimed control of her destiny but also discovered a profound sense of purpose and fulfilment that transcended monetary success. Her journey serves as a beacon of inspiration for women who find themselves trapped in similar situations, seeking validation from external sources and society's expectations.

Maya's story teaches us that life planning is not a luxury reserved for the privileged few; it's a necessity for anyone seeking true fulfilment and happiness. By delving deep into our values, passions and aspirations, we can unlock the doors to a life rich in purpose, meaning and authenticity.

For women who feel stuck in the rut of convention and expectation, Maya's journey offers a powerful lesson: it's never too late to rewrite your narrative, redefine success on your own terms and pursue your dreams with unwavering courage and conviction.

In embracing life planning, we empower ourselves to seize control of our destinies, make decisions that resonate with our deepest desires and embark on journeys of self-discovery and empowerment. Maya's journey reminds us that the path to true fulfilment begins with the courage to listen to our hearts, trust in our inner voice and daring to live authentically, unapologetically and with purpose.

The Ideal Lifestyle and How to Achieve It

We now delve deeper into the concept of the ideal lifestyle and how women, like Renu, can take concrete steps to achieve it. The ideal lifestyle is not a one-size-fits-all concept; rather, it's deeply personal and unique to each individual. It encompasses not only financial success but also emotional well-being, personal growth and meaningful connections. It's about living a life that aligns with your values, passions and aspirations.

Renu's story exemplifies the timeless struggle faced by many women: the delicate balancing act between career aspirations and familial responsibilities. As a devoted mother and dedicated professional, Renu found herself caught in this perpetual tug-of-war, yearning for harmony and fulfilment in both spheres of her life.

For Renu, the ideal lifestyle wasn't just about achieving professional success or fulfilling familial duties; it was about finding a harmonious balance between the two while also prioritising her well-being and personal growth.

One of the key principles of life planning is aligning financial decisions with personal values. It's about understanding what truly matters to you and using money as a tool to support those values and aspirations. Achieving the ideal lifestyle requires taking charge of your financial life and reclaiming the power to make life choices. It's about recognising that financial independence is not just about accumulating wealth but about having the autonomy to live life on your own terms.

Life planning has transformative power in empowering women to chart their paths and cultivate lives rich in purpose and authenticity. By prioritising values, aspirations and personal growth, women can transcend societal expectations and redefine success on their terms.

Ultimately, achieving the ideal lifestyle is about unlocking the greatest meaning and fulfilment in your life. It's about living authentically, pursuing your passions and creating a life that resonates with your deepest desires.

Money and Sacrifice

Money holds a significant place in our lives, but its value extends beyond mere currency. In this section, we explore the profound concept of sacrifice and the pivotal role it plays in the pursuit of women's dreams and aspirations. Through poignant anecdotes, we illuminate the courageous decisions and trade-offs women often face in their quest for personal and professional fulfilment.

For many women, achieving their goals requires sacrifices—be it relinquishing a high-paying career to pursue their passion, downsizing their lifestyle to prioritise experiences over material possessions or making tough financial choices to align with long-term aspirations. These sacrifices embody a willingness to forego immediate gratification in favour of long-term fulfilment and purpose.

By sharing the stories of women who have embraced such sacrifices, we honour their resilience and determination to carve out lives that reflect their authentic selves. These narratives serve as powerful reminders that true wealth lies not in material possessions but in the richness of experiences, relationships and personal growth.

Through the lens of sacrifice, we invite each one of you to reflect on your own journey and consider the trade-offs you are willing to make in pursuit of your dreams. By embracing the challenges and uncertainties that accompany such decisions, we women can forge paths that are guided by authenticity, passion and a profound sense of purpose.

Life Planning for a Fulfilling Future

Let's transition from introspection to action with practical guidance on creating a comprehensive life plan that aligns with your aspirations and values. Drawing upon the insights we've discussed, let's craft a roadmap to guide you towards a future characterised by fulfilment, abundance and authenticity.

At the heart of effective life planning lies a deep understanding of yourself—your motivations, desires and priorities. It's about embarking on a journey of self-discovery, where you take the time to reflect on what truly matters to you and what you envision for your future.

To begin this journey, carve out moments of introspection. Whether through journalling, meditation or deep conversations with trusted confidants, allow yourself the space to explore your personal values, passions and long-term aspirations. These moments lay the foundation for the life plan ahead.

Next, articulate clear goals and aspirations. Envision your ideal future across various aspects of life—career, relationships, personal growth, health and leisure. Ensure these goals are specific, measurable, achievable, relevant and time-bound (SMART), providing you with a roadmap for progress and accountability.

Equally crucial is evaluating your financial resources and developing a strategic plan to achieve your life goals. Take a proactive approach to your finances by assessing your current financial situation—income, expenses, assets and liabilities.

Budgeting emerges as a fundamental tool in financial planning. Allocate your resources in alignment with your priorities and goals. By tracking expenses and identifying areas for optimisation, you can maximise your financial resources and accelerate progress towards your aspirations.

Saving becomes a cornerstone of financial stability and future planning. Cultivate a habit of saving regularly, setting aside a portion of your income for short-term needs, emergencies and long-term goals such as retirement or education funding.

Investing offers an opportunity to grow wealth over time. Explore various investment vehicles suited to your risk tolerance, time horizon and financial objectives. From stocks and bonds to real estate and mutual funds, the investment landscape offers diverse options for wealth accumulation and preservation.

Managing debt is another critical aspect of financial planning. Approach debt with a strategic mindset, understanding the implications of borrowing and developing a plan to pay down debt systematically while minimising interest costs.

As you embark on your life planning journey, remember that the path to fulfilment is not always linear or predictable. It requires courage, resilience and a willingness to adapt to changing circumstances. However, by embracing the principles of life planning and financial planning, you can navigate the complexities of modern life with confidence and clarity, secure in the knowledge that you are charting your own course towards a future that is uniquely yours.

With determination and purpose, may you embark on this journey of self-discovery and empowerment, paving the way for a life rich in meaning, authenticity and fulfilment.

Financial Planning the Smart Way— The Why, How and What

'Financial freedom is available to those who learn about it and work for it.'

—Robert Kiyosaki

FINANCIAL PLANNING IS OFTEN PERCEIVED AS COMPLEX AND RESERVED for the wealthy or deemed unnecessary by those who consider themselves successful. However, just as everyone needs medical treatment regardless of wealth or success, financial planning is essential for all individuals, regardless of their financial status.

Financial planning is about utilising your financial resources effectively to achieve your goals, ensuring you're on the right path to financial security and independence.

Let's explore the smart way of financial planning—the why, how and what behind it.

Women have always been the backbone of society, juggling multiple roles as mothers, wives, daughters and professionals.

However, despite their indispensable contributions, women often face unique financial challenges, such as having a smaller income, taking career breaks and outliving men. These challenges underscore the importance of having a well-defined financial plan to ensure women's financial security and ability to meet their goals.

The Why—The importance of having a purpose: Financial planning begins with understanding your purpose. It defines your relationship with money and guides you as you focus on the how and what of financial planning. Whether it's safety, security, financial independence or freedom, your purpose acts as a compass, aligning your goals and actions with your values and aspirations.

For example, consider a woman who values financial independence and aims to be debt-free. Her purpose, is clear—to achieve financial independence and eliminate debt. This purpose guides her as she sets financial goals and creates a plan to achieve them.

The How—Achieving goals: Once you've established your purpose, it's time to focus on the how—the process of achieving your goals. This involves setting realistic and achievable financial goals, creating a budget, managing debt, saving for emergencies and investing for the future. Having a structured approach to financial planning ensures you can effectively navigate towards your goals.

For instance, if your goal is to become debt-free, your how will involve creating a budget conducive to paying off debts faster, negotiating with creditors for lower interest rates and exploring debt consolidation options to streamline payments, which would involve combining multiple debts into a single, more manageable payment. This can be achieved through various methods, each with its own benefits and considerations.

The What—Choosing the right financial products: Choosing the right financial products is essential for achieving your goals effectively. The what involves selecting products that align with your needs, goals and risk appetite. Your chosen products will determine the success of your financial plan and how well you can achieve your goals.

For example, if your goal is to save for retirement, your what would entail choosing the right investments that align with your objectives. Building a diversified portfolio tailored to your risk tolerance and time horizon is key to securing a comfortable retirement.

The Smart Way is a powerful tool for achieving financial goals. By starting with your purpose and aligning your strategy with your values, you can create a plan that leads to financial independence, security and freedom. Seeking guidance from a financial advisor can help you choose the right financial products and stay on track towards your goals over the long term. Just as a doctor offers a diagnosis before prescribing medication, financial planning begins with understanding your goals and aspirations before selecting the right financial products.

Section 4

The Financially Smart Seven-Month Action Plan

The Financially Smart Seven-Month Action Plan is where the rubber meets the road. It is an essential section that will guide you through a seven-month plan to help you implement the financial planning concepts you have learnt in the previous chapter.

For every month, we will focus on a specific financial topic and provide you with a checklist of tasks to complete. These tasks will help you create a solid foundation for your financial future and build momentum towards achieving your financial goals.

- ✓ Month 1: Set up your bank account and get a handle on your cashflows.
- ✓ Month 2: Build your personal financial statement (cashflow and net worth statement).
- ✓ Month 3: Create your SMART Money Management Accounting System.
- ✓ Month 4: Set SMART financial goals and create a plan to achieve them.
- ✓ Month 5: Your lifeline in testing times—build your emergency fund and risk management plan.
- ✓ Month 6: Start saving and investing towards your goals, including retirement.

✓ Month 7: The journey continues—review your progress and make necessary changes. (Fix a quarterly money date with yourself.)

By the end of this section, you will have a customised financial plan that suits your unique needs and goals. You will be equipped with the knowledge and tools to take control of your financial future and become a financially smart woman. So, let us get started and take the first step towards financial freedom!

Month 1: Set Up Your Bank Account and Get a Handle on Your Cash Flows

'A good financial plan is a road map that shows us exactly how the choices we make today will affect our future.'
—Alexa Von Tobel

FINANCIAL INDEPENDENCE IS A CRUCIAL STEP TOWARDS ACHIEVING overall independence, especially for women. One of the first and most important steps towards financial independence is having your own bank account. It not only gives you the freedom to manage your finances but also helps in building a sense of confidence in your abilities.

Having your bank account means having complete control over your finances. You have the power to decide how much to save, invest or spend. It is essential to learn how to operate your bank account efficiently, which includes using net banking, debit cards and chequebooks or creating and breaking fixed deposits. By learning these basics, you equip yourself with the necessary skills to manage your finances independently.

Putting money into your account is the next step towards building a financially secure future. Whether it is your salary, business earnings or even a gift or allowance, make it a point to transfer whatever money you receive into your account. This not only helps you keep track of your finances but also enables you to start building a healthy financial reserve for yourself.

In addition to setting up your bank account, it's also crucial to create one of the most important statements— your Cashflow Statement, which consolidates your income and tracking your expenses from every possible source. You can decide on the timeframe you take for capturing this information. In the example below, we have considered it as a financial year from 1 April 2024 to 31 March 2025. If you find it challenging to predict next year's income, you can use last year's income as a reference and adjust it based on your current situation.

This process varies depending on your profession. Salaried workers usually have a steady income, while self-employed individuals may experience fluctuations.

This statement highlights areas for improvement and helps you stay on top of your finances. It helps you make prudent choices of the surplus funds, if any, and helps you allocate them towards your personal financial goals, thus giving you a handle on your financial situation. If there is a negative cashflow or no surplus, then this statement and its ratios work as an eye opener and point out problem areas that you can work on.

Track your expenses regularly using tools like budgeting apps or simple spreadsheets to make informed financial decisions and adjust your spending habits as needed.

Step-by-Step Guide to Opening a Bank Account

1. *Research*: Research different banks to find one that meets your needs. Look for factors such as interest rates, fees, ATM access, online banking services and customer service ratings. You can also ask for recommendations from friends and family members.

2. *Choose an account type*: Once you have chosen a bank, select the type of account you want to open. The most common types of accounts include savings accounts, current accounts and fixed deposit accounts.

   1. *Savings accounts*: Savings accounts are one of the most common types of bank accounts and are designed for storing money while earning interest. They typically offer easy access to funds, allowing you to deposit and withdraw money as needed. They are ideal for individuals looking to build an emergency fund, save for short-term goals or simply keep their money safe while earning a modest interest.

   2. *Current accounts*: Also known as checking accounts, these are designed for frequent transactions and daily banking needs. They offer features such as cheque-writing capabilities, debit cards and overdraft protection, making them suitable for individuals or businesses with high transaction volumes.

   3. *Fixed deposit accounts*: Fixed deposit accounts, also known as time deposit accounts, are investment vehicles that offer higher interest rates in exchange for locking in funds for a specified period. These accounts are ideal for individuals looking to earn higher returns on their savings while maintaining a predetermined level of liquidity.

Account Type	Return	Taxation	Liquidity
Savings Account	Modest interest rates	Interest may be taxable	High; easy access
Current Account	No interest	No interest earned; subject to service charges	High; unlimited transactions
Fixed Deposit Account	Higher interest rates	Interest may be taxable	Low; funds locked in for a fixed term

3. *Gather required documents*: To open a bank account, you will typically need to provide the following documents:
    1. Proof of identity: Aadhaar card; passport; Voter ID card; driving license; PAN card (Permanent Account Number)
    2. Proof of address: Aadhaar card; passport; voter ID card; utility bills (electricity, water, gas) issued within the last three months; bank or post office passbook with address details; rental agreement
    3. Passport-size photographs: Usually, two photographs are required.
    4. Additional documents (if applicable):
        - Income proof documents (such as salary slips, income tax returns) may be required for certain types of accounts or if you wish to apply for overdraft facilities or credit products.
        - For non-resident Indian (NRI) accounts, additional documents such as proof of foreign address, employment details and passport with visa may be required.

Check with the specific bank for their exact requirements and any additional documents they may need for account opening. Additionally, some banks may have online account opening facilities where you can electronically submit scanned copies of documents. Gather these documents before you visit the bank so that you can produce them when required. This will save you unnecessary trips to the bank and will help your work to get done quickly.

4. *Visit the bank*: Once you have gathered all the required documents, visit the nearest branch of the bank where you wish to open an account. Ask the customer service or banking representative for an account opening form.

    Fill in all the required details accurately on the form. Ensure that you provide correct information as per the supporting documents you are submitting.

    Submit the completed form along with the necessary documents to the bank representative. They will verify the details provided and may ask for any additional information if required.

    Alternatively, if you have a relationship manager (RM) assigned to you or if you are dealing with the bank through a personal banker, you may contact them directly. Your RM can assist you with the account opening process and may even arrange to collect the necessary documents from your location for added convenience.

    By visiting the bank in person or contacting your RM, you can ensure a smooth account opening process and get your queries or concerns you may have regarding the procedure clarified.

5. *Fund the account*: Once your account is opened, the next step is to fund it. You need to deposit some initial funds

to activate your account. You can choose from various methods to deposit funds, including transferring money from an existing account, depositing cash, using a cheque or leveraging digital payment platforms like Google Pay.

Putting money into your account is not just a routine task; it's a crucial step towards building a financially secure future. Whether it's your salary, business earnings or even a gift or allowance, transferring funds into your account helps you keep track of your finances and start building a healthy financial reserve.

Moreover, opening a bank account offers you access to a range of financial tools and benefits that can enhance your banking experience and financial management:

- *Debit card*: A debit card linked to your bank account allows you to make purchases online and at retail stores, withdraw cash from ATMs and conduct various banking transactions conveniently.

- *Cheque book*: Most banks provide a cheque book when you open an account, enabling you to issue cheques for payments and transactions.

- *Passbook*: A passbook serves as a record of your account transactions. It provides details of deposits, withdrawals and account balances, helping you track your financial activities.

- *Internet banking*: Many banks offer internet banking facilities, allowing you to manage your account online. With internet banking, you can check your account balance, transfer funds, pay bills and perform other banking transactions from the comfort of your home or office.

- *Digital payment platforms*: Utilising digital payment platforms like Google Pay adds convenience to your banking experience. You can easily transfer money to friends and family, pay bills, recharge mobile phones and make online purchases using your linked bank account.

By leveraging these banking tools and services, you can streamline your financial activities, track your expenses and manage your money more efficiently. Ultimately, having a bank account and managing it effectively empowers you to take control of your finances and work towards financial independence. So, seize the opportunity today and take the first step toward a financially secure future.

Action Points

- *Identify your expenses*: Start by making a comprehensive list of all your expenses. Differentiate between fixed expenses, such as rent, loan EMIs and insurance premiums and variable expenses, such as groceries, transportation and entertainment.

- *Choose a tracking method*: Decide on a tracking method that suits your preferences and lifestyle. You can opt for a budgeting app like Monefy, Walnut, Money View, ET Money, Expense Manager or use a spreadsheet on your computer, or simply jot down expenses using pen and paper.

- *Categorise your expenses*: Group your expenses into categories to gain insights into your spending habits. Typical categories include essentials like housing and food and other expenses such as transportation, entertainment and miscellaneous expenses. This classification helps you pinpoint where you might cut costs and manage your resources more effectively. Remember, expenses can be classified as mandatory (necessary), fixed or variable, giving you a clearer picture of your financial commitments and flexibility.

- *Set a budget*: Based on your expenses and income, establish a budget for each category. Determine a set amount that you aim not to exceed for each expense category. Ensure that your total expenses do not exceed your total income, leaving room for savings and unexpected expenses.

- *Track your expenses*: Regularly track your expenses, whether it's on a weekly or monthly basis, to stay informed about your spending habits. Consistently reviewing your spending helps you stay within your budget and make necessary adjustments as needed.

By following these steps, you can establish a system for tracking your expenses and gain a clear understanding of your financial situation. This foundational step is crucial for taking control of your finances and working towards achieving your financial goals. Once you have a firm grasp of your expenses and income, you can proceed to build a personal income/cash flow statement, which outlines what comes into your account and what goes out, followed by a net worth statement to assess your overall financial health.

Month 2: Build Your Personal Financial Statement— Cashflow and Net Worth Statement

'The goal isn't more money. The goal is living life on your terms.'
—Chris Brogan

WELCOME TO MONTH 2 OF YOUR FINANCIALLY SMART BLUEPRINT Action Plan. In this chapter, we'll guide you through the process of building your personal financial statement—your cashflow and net worth statements.

Cash Flow Statement

Start by creating a cash flow statement to track the flow of money into and out of your accounts over a specific period, typically a month. This statement helps you understand your spending patterns and how much cash you have on hand after meeting your expenses.

- *Income*: List all sources of income, including salary, bonuses, side hustle earnings, rental income, dividends, etc. Be sure to include both your net income (after taxes) and any additional income streams.
- *Expenses*: Refer back to the comprehensive list of expenses you created in Month 1. Record all your expenses under their respective categories, distinguishing between fixed and variable expenses.
- *Net cash flow*: Calculate the net cash flow by subtracting your total expenses from your total income. A positive cash flow indicates that you have more money coming in than going out, while a negative cash flow signals that you're spending more than you earn.

Regularly review your cash flow statement to identify spending patterns, areas where you can save and opportunities to increase your income.

Sample Cash Flow Statement for Maya

Category	Amount (₹) Monthly	Amount (₹) Annually
Income		
Salary	4,00,000	48,00,000
Consulting Income	0	0
Rental Income	0	0
Interest Income	5,000	60,000
Total Income	405000	4860000

Category	Amount (₹) Monthly	Amount (₹) Annually
Expenses		
Mandatory Fixed Expenses		
Home Loan EMI	65,000	7,80,000
Car Loan EMI	30,000	3,60,000
Insurance Premiums	15,000	1,80,000
Total Mandatory Expenses	1,10,000	13,20,000
Variable Expenses		
Groceries	12,000	1,44,000
House Help Salary	20,000	2,40,000
Travel	18,000	2,16,000
Investments	30,000	3,60,000
Entertainment	25,000	3,00,000
Medical Expenses	10,000	1,20,000
Gym/Membership Fees	5,000	60,000
All Utility Bills (Electricity, Gas, Internet, etc.)	20,000	2,40,000
Clothing/Personal Care	22,000	2,64,000
Dining Out	18,000	2,16,000

Category	Amount (₹) Monthly	Amount (₹) Annually
Shopping	21,000	2,52,000
Total Variable Expenses	2,01,000	24,12,000
Total Expenses	3,11,000	37,32,000
Net Cash Flow	**94,000**	**11,28,000**

The net cash flow is calculated as the difference between total income and total expenses: **Net Cash Flow = Total Income - Total Expenses**

Net Monthly Cash Flow = 4,05,000 – 3,11,000 = ₹**94,000**

Net Annual Cash Flow = 48,60,000 – 37,32,000 = ₹**11,28,000**

This means that Maya's net cash flow is positive, and the amount is available for savings and can be directed towards growing her wealth.

Building Your Net Worth Statement

Understanding your net worth is crucial for financial planning as it provides a snapshot of your financial health by assessing the relationship between your assets and liabilities. We will now guide you through the process of creating your net worth statement, helping you gain insights into your financial situation and set realistic goals.

A net worth statement is a financial document that calculates the difference between your total assets and total liabilities.

It provides a clear picture of your current financial standing, indicating whether you have more assets than liabilities (positive net worth) or vice versa (negative net worth).

Step 1: List Your Assets (A)

Assets are items of value that you own, ranging from cash to investments and properties. Here's how to list your assets:

1. *Cash*: Include the total amount of cash you have in hand and in your savings accounts. For example:
    - Savings Account: ₹3,00,000
    - Fixed Deposits: ₹10,00,000
    - Cash: ₹30,000

2. *Investments*: Record the current market value of your investments, such as stocks, mutual funds and retirement accounts.
    For example:
    - Stocks: ₹10,000
    - Mutual Funds: ₹2,00,000
    - Public Provident Fund (PPF): ₹50,000
    - LIC Cash Value: ₹2,00,000

3. *Property*: Estimate the current market value of any real estate you own, subtracting any outstanding loans.
    - Residential Property: ₹40,00,000

4. *Vehicles*: Determine the value of your vehicles, considering depreciation.
    - Car: ₹5,00,000

5. *Jewellery*: Determine the value of your jewellery.
    * Jewellery: ₹2,00,000

6. *Total assets (A)*: Sum up the values of all your assets. With
    the sample values we have taken:
    * Total Assets (A) = ₹64,90,000

Step 2: List Your Liabilities (B)

Liabilities represent the debts you owe, including loans and
credit card balances. Here's how to list your liabilities:

1. *Home loan*: Include the remaining balance of any mortgage
    or home loan. For example:
    * Remaining Balance: ₹30,00,000

2. *Car loan*: Record the remaining balance of any car loans.
    For example:
    * Remaining Balance: ₹5,00,000

3. *Credit card debt*: Sum up any outstanding balances on your
    credit cards. For example:
    * Visa: ₹90,000
    * Mastercard: ₹35,000

4. *Personal loan*: ₹2,00,000

5. *Total liabilities (B):* Calculate the total value of your
    liabilities.
    * Total Liabilities (B) = ₹38,25,000

Step 3: Calculate Your Net Worth

To calculate your net worth, subtract your total liabilities (B) from your total assets (A):

- Net Worth = Total Assets (A) - Total Liabilities (B)
- Net Worth = ₹64,90,000 - ₹38,25,000
- **Net Worth = ₹26,65,000**

Sample Net Worth Statement of Maya

Net Worth Statement as on 31 March 2024					
LIABILITIES (in Rs)			**ASSETS (in Rs)**		
		Ms Maya			**Ms Maya**
Current Liabilities			**Cash/Near Cash (Liquid Assets)**		
1	Credit Card	1,25,000	1	Savings A/C	3,00,000
2	Home Loan	30,00,000	2	Bank FD	10,00,000
3	Car Loan	5,00,000	3	Liquid Fund	
4	Personal Loan	2,00,000	4	Cash	30,000
5	Any other Liabilities			**Total**	13,30,000
			Invested Assets (approx. market value)		
			1	Stock/Shares	10,000
			2	Equity Mutual Funds	2,00,000
			3	Life Insurance Cash Value	2,00,000
			4	Debt Mutual Funds	
			5	Bonds	
			6	PPF	50,000

Net Worth Statement as on 31 March 2024					
LIABILITIES (in Rs)			**ASSETS (in Rs)**		
			7	NPS	
			8	Sr. Citizen Saving Scheme	
			9	Private Equity	
			10	Real Estate	
			11	Gold (Physical/ ETFs)	-
			12	Real Estate PMS	-
				Total	**4,60,000**
			Personal/Lifestyle Assets (approx. market value)		
			1	Residential Home	40,00,000
			2	Car	5,00,000
			3	Jewellery	2,00,000
				Total	**47,00,000**
Total Liabilities	**38,25,000**		**Total Assets**		**64,90,000**
Total Net Worth = Total Assets - Total Liabilities					**26,65,000**

Review and Adjust

Regularly review your net worth statement to track your financial progress. Identify areas where you can increase assets, decrease liabilities or adjust your financial strategy to improve your net worth over time.

By creating and updating your net worth statement, you gain valuable insights into your financial health and progress towards your financial goals. It serves as a foundational tool for making informed financial decisions and achieving long-term financial stability.

Maya's net worth as of 31 March 2024 is ₹26,65,000. This positive net worth indicates that her assets exceed her liabilities. However, she realises that she has room for improvement, especially in reducing debt and increasing savings and investments.

Regularly update your net worth statement to track changes in your financial situation and progress towards your goals.

Let's start building your financial statement to take control of your finances and secure your future.

By the end of Month 2, you will have a clear understanding of your net worth and be able to track your financial progress. In the next chapter, we will focus on setting financial goals and creating a plan to achieve them.

Action Points

1. Collect all your financial documents and organise them in one place.
2. Use the template provided in this chapter to create your financial statement.
3. Calculate your net worth by subtracting your total liabilities from your total assets.
4. Analyse your net worth and identify areas that need improvement.
5. Set a goal to increase your net worth by a specific amount in the next six months.

Month 3: Mastering Your Finances with the Smart Money Management Model

'You must gain control over your money or the lack of it will forever control you.'

—Dave Ramsey

WELCOME TO THE WORLD OF FINANCIAL EMPOWERMENT, WHERE managing your money becomes a journey of clarity, control and prosperity. As it is rightly said, it's not just about how much money you make, but what you keep from what you make.

In this month, we will learn to implement the Smart Money Management Accounting System—a dynamic approach that adapts to your financial goals and lifestyle, making financial management not just a task but a strategic and empowering habit. Before we look at the implementation, let us quickly review the model.

The Smart Money Management Model

Check your cashflow statement and divide the total income received into your salary or income account into the following two parts to start off, so that you are not dipping into your Essentials Account once you have parked it aside. Instead of jars which we have spoken about in a previous chapter, I am replacing it here with plastic envelopes for ease and convenience.

1. *Essentials Account—Necessities Envelope (50%)*: Your primary spending account, e.g., rent, utilities, groceries and transportation.

2. *Growth Account*: Your main savings account can be further divided into five specialised accounts: You have an option here to use plastic envelopes that can be purchased from any stationery shop with name tags to keep the amounts (if the cash amount is not too much). You can also park it into five different bank accounts:

   - *Long-term Savings for Spending Towards the Goals Envelope: 10%*
     Dedicated to funding your short- and long-term SMART goals. Invest based on your planned time frame.
   - *Financial Freedom Envelope: 10%*
     Reserved for building long-term financial freedom. Never spend this money except in emergencies after utilising the emergency fund.
   - *Personal Development Envelope: 10%*
     Invest in acquiring more knowledge and skills that can increase your earning capacity.

- *Play Envelope: 10%*
  Use this to spend without guilt, pamper yourself and reward yourself too.

- *Giving Envelope: 5%*
  Use this envelope to invest in charities and help others, fostering a sense of abundance and satisfaction.

(Remember the percentages have been given as an estimate. Feel free to divide the amounts as a percentage based on your individual situation.)

Action Points

Follow these steps to effectively implement the model in your life:

1. *Start small and build the habit:* Begin by allocating the suggested percentages to each envelope. Start with an amount you can manage, and gradually increase it as you become comfortable.
2. *Automate your finances:* Set up automatic transfers to each envelope using online banking features or financial management apps. This ensures a disciplined approach to your financial goals.
3. *Regularly review and adjust:* Regularly review your allocations and adjust them based on changes in your financial situation or goals. Flexibility is key to adapting this system to your evolving needs.

Case Study 1: Transformative Financial Journey

We introduced Maya to the Smart Money Management Model, and she embraced it with great success.

1. *Necessities Envelope: 40%*
   - Allocating 40% of her income to the Essentials Account, or Necessities Envelope, demonstrates Maya's commitment to ensuring stability and security in her financial life. By dedicating a significant portion of her income to cover essential needs, Maya establishes a solid foundation upon which she can build her financial well-being.
   - This envelope serves as a safety net, providing Maya with the means to meet her basic necessities such as housing, food, utilities, transportation and healthcare. By prioritising essential expenses, Maya ensures that she can maintain a comfortable standard of living and safeguard herself against financial hardship.
   - By allocating almost half of her income to the Essentials Account, Maya demonstrates responsible financial management and prioritises her well-being and security. This envelope forms the cornerstone of her financial plan, allowing her to navigate through life's uncertainties with confidence and resilience.

2. *Goals Envelope: 20%*
   - Setting aside 20% of her income to the Goals Envelope has empowered Maya to turn her dreams into reality. This envelope serves as a dedicated fund to finance her aspirations, whether it's embarking on her dream

vacation, purchasing her dream car or kickstarting a side business.

- By allocating a significant portion of her financial resources to her goals, Maya demonstrates her commitment to realising her ambitions and creating the life she desires. This envelope provides her with the financial means to pursue her dreams with confidence and determination.

- By prioritising her goals and allocating funds accordingly, Maya is actively shaping her future and laying the foundation for a life filled with fulfilment and success.

3. *Financial Freedom Envelope: 15%*
   - Maya's commitment to allocating 15% of her income to the Financial Freedom Envelope is a proactive step towards securing her financial future. This envelope serves as a cornerstone in the Smart Money Management Model, providing her with a tool to save for the long term and achieve financial freedom.

   - The 'Fill it, Shut it, Forget it' approach underscores the importance of consistency and discipline in Maya's investment strategy. Once she sets aside funds for this envelope, she can trust in its growth over time, allowing her to focus on other aspects of her financial journey.

   - Regular contributions to the Financial Freedom Envelope create a safety net for Maya, giving her the flexibility to pursue her goals and aspirations without being constrained by financial worries. This envelope symbolises Maya's commitment to financial independence and serves as a key component of her path towards a prosperous future.

4. *Education Envelope: 10%*
   - Allocating 10% of her income to the Education Envelope reflects Maya's commitment to personal and professional growth. By investing in online courses and workshops, Maya actively seeks to enhance her skills, broaden her knowledge, and explore new career opportunities.
   - The Education Envelope serves as a dedicated fund to support Maya's continuous learning journey. Whether she's acquiring new skills relevant to her current profession or exploring new fields of interest, Maya's investment in education enables her to stay relevant in a rapidly evolving job market and positions her for career advancement.
   - By upgrading her skills and knowledge through educational investments, Maya not only increases her earning potential but also opens doors to new possibilities and opportunities for personal and professional development. This envelope represents Maya's proactive approach to self-improvement and her commitment to realising her full potential.

5. *Play Envelope: 10%*
   - Allocating 10% of her income to the Play Envelope has allowed Maya to indulge in life's pleasures guilt-free. This envelope allows her to pamper herself and enjoy experiences that bring joy and fulfilment to her life.
   - Whether it's treating herself to a spa day, planning a night out with friends or splurging on a lovely bag, Maya's Play Envelope enables both financial responsibility and personal enjoyment.

- By consciously setting aside funds for leisure and enjoyment, Maya fosters a sense of well-being and happiness in her life. This envelope not only adds richness to her experiences but also contributes to her overall satisfaction and fulfilment.

6. *Giving Envelope: 5%*
   - Allocating 5% of her income to the Giving Envelope has enabled Maya to make meaningful contributions to local charities, thereby fostering a sense of community and gratitude.
   - By dedicating a portion of her financial resources to giving back, Maya not only supports causes that are important to her but also enriches the lives of others in her community. Her contributions help address pressing social issues and make a positive impact on the lives of those in need.
   - Engaging in philanthropy through the Giving Envelope allows Maya to cultivate a spirit of generosity and empathy, strengthening her connection to her community and instilling a sense of fulfilment derived from making a difference in the lives of others.
   - Through her contributions to local charities, Maya embodies the values of compassion and altruism, leaving a lasting legacy of kindness and goodwill in her community.

Through disciplined adherence to the Smart Money Management Model, Maya not only achieved her financial goals but also found a sense of financial security and empowerment.

Now, let's explore how this system can be applied in a real-life scenario, for couples or partners moving in together who plan their finances.

Case Study 2: Smart Life Account for Couples

Meet Rahul and Priya, a couple with a combined monthly income of ₹1,00,000. They've embraced the Smart Money Management Model to manage their finances effectively.

- *Common Daily Necessities Account: ₹60,000 (60%)*
  A joint account for shared daily expenses, based on mutually agreed proportions of their earnings.

- *Individual Spending Accounts: ₹20,000 each (20% each)*
  Each partner maintains a personal spending account for discretionary expenses.

- *Investment Account: Remaining Balance*
  Both Rahul and Priya transfer any remaining funds from their individual spending accounts into the joint investment account.

  They tried this out for a couple of months and then started transferring the amount from the next month as per the percentages they worked on individually into their Financial Freedom, Long-term Savings and Spending for Goals, Education, Play and Give Accounts.

For the first few months, they used physical envelopes or a simple spreadsheet to manually allocate funds. As they became more comfortable with the system, they gradually automated the process using online banking features.

During an unexpected medical expense, Rahul and Priya had to dip into their joint investment account. Because they had built a robust system, this temporary setback didn't disrupt their overall financial plan. As they continued to automate their finances, they were able to replenish the joint investment account and maintain their financial stability.

The Smart Money Management Model: Simplify, Automate, Reap, Transform

Managing your money is a crucial life skill that requires constant attention and discipline. The Smart Money Management Model is an automated accounting system designed to provide a roadmap to financial well-being.

Start small by implementing this method into your daily routine. Automate your finances to ensure consistency and efficiency. As you adopt this healthy and wealthy system and make it a regular habit, you're not just simplifying your finances, you're building a corpus for a prosperous future.

Remember, financial empowerment is a journey, and with each step, you're transforming your financial landscape. Whether you're an individual or part of a couple, this system provides clarity, control and a path to enduring financial well-being.

Month 4: Set SMART Financial Goals and Create a Plan to Achieve Them

'A goal without a plan is just a wish.'
—Antoine de Saint-Exupéry

As we move into Month 4 of our financial action plan, it's time to set some financial goals and create a plan to achieve them.

Remember the SMART approach to goal setting? It stands for specific, measurable, achievable, relevant and time-bound. Using this framework, we can create financial goals that are clear, focused and achievable.

Step 1: Identify Your Financial Goals

The first step is to identify your financial goals. Ask yourself: What do I want to achieve financially? Do I want to pay off debt, save for a down payment on a house, build an emergency fund or invest in my retirement? Whatever your financial goals are, write them down and make sure they are specific, measurable, achievable, relevant and time-bound.

For example, let's say your goal is to pay off your credit card debt of ₹50,000 within the next twelve months. This goal is specific (pay off credit card debt), measurable (₹50,000), achievable (within twelve months), relevant (reducing debt) and time-bound (twelve months).

Step 2: Create an Action Plan

Once you have identified your financial goals, the next step is to create an action plan. Your action plan should include the specific steps you need to take to achieve your financial goals. To pay off your credit card debt of INR 50,000 within the next twelve months, your action plan might look like this:

1. *Analyse your budget*: Look at your budget and see where you can cut back on expenses. This will free up extra cash to put towards paying off your debt.
2. *Increase your income*: Look for ways to increase your income, such as taking on a part-time job, freelancing or selling items you no longer need.
3. *Create a debt repayment plan*: Decide on a strategy for paying off your credit card debt. One approach is to prioritise paying off the card with the highest interest rate first while making minimum payments on the others. Once that card is paid off, move on to the card with the next highest interest rate.
4. *Stick to your budget*: It's important to stick to your budget and avoid unnecessary expenses. This will help you stay on track with your debt repayment plan.

5. *Monitor your progress*: Keep track of your progress by regularly checking your credit card balances and debt repayment plan. Celebrate small milestones along the way to stay motivated.

Step 3: Identify Potential Obstacles

No matter what your financial goals are, there will always be potential obstacles that could get in the way. It's important to identify these obstacles and come up with strategies for overcoming them. For example, some potential obstacles to paying off your credit card debt might include unexpected expenses such as a medical emergency, job loss or a decrease in income. Strategies for overcoming these obstacles might include building an emergency fund, looking for additional sources of income or reducing your expenses even further.

Step 4: Take Action

Now that you have identified your financial goals, created an action plan and identified potential obstacles, it's time to take action. Remember, the key to achieving your financial goals is to stay committed and disciplined. Keep track of your progress, adjust your action plan as needed and celebrate your successes along the way.

- *Month 1*: Review your credit card statements and create a budget to track your expenses.
- *Month 2*: Cut back on unnecessary expenses and use the extra money to make a larger credit card payment.

- *Month 3*: Negotiate a lower interest rate with your credit card company.
- *Month 4–12*: Continue to make larger payments each month until your debt is paid off.

Remember, financial goal setting is an ongoing process. As you achieve your goals, you may need to set new ones or adjust your existing ones. The key is to stay focused, stay motivated and continue taking steps towards achieving your financial dreams.

Let's look at some examples of common financial goals and how to go about meeting them:

- *Paying off student loans*: Let's say you have a student loan debt of INR 2,00,000, and your goal is to pay it off in the next five years. To achieve this goal, you can create an action plan that includes paying more than the minimum amount due each month, negotiating a lower interest rate with your lender and finding additional sources of income while trying to find the highest-paying job possible at your skill and experience level. Potential obstacles might include unexpected expenses or a decrease in income, but by having a solid action plan in place, you can overcome these obstacles and achieve your goal of being debt-free.
- *Saving for retirement*: Saving for retirement demands a proactive approach. Begin by crafting a meticulous budget to monitor your expenses closely. Identify areas where you can trim unnecessary spending, channelling those funds towards retirement savings. Next, establish a robust savings plan, setting aside a consistent portion of your income for retirement. Consider exploring retirement investment options such to maximise your savings potential. Regularly

reassess your financial goals and adjust your retirement savings strategy accordingly to ensure you're on track to achieve a secure and comfortable retirement.

Action Points

Setting smart financial goals is a critical step in achieving financial independence. Here's an actionable plan for Month 4 to help you set your financial goals:

1. *Determine your financial goals*: Review your financial goals. Consider your life stage, income and personal priorities.
2. *Set specific and measurable goals*: Once you have identified your financial goals, break them down into specific and measurable targets. For example, if your goal is to buy a house, determine how much you need for a down payment, closing costs and ongoing mortgage payments.
3. *Prioritise your goals*: It's important to prioritise your goals based on their importance and urgency. For example, if you have children who will be going to college soon, saving for their education may be a higher priority than saving for retirement.
4. *Determine your timeline*: Set a realistic timeline for achieving your financial goals. Determine how much you need to save each month to reach your targets within your set timeframe.
5. *Identify investment options*: Once you know how much you need to save and for how long, explore investment

options that can help you reach your goals. Consider a mix of investments that provide growth potential and stability, such as mutual funds, stocks and bonds.

Remember, financial goals are personal and can vary based on individual circumstances. The key is to set specific and achievable goals that align with your priorities and values. By following a SMART goal-setting plan, you can take control of your finances and achieve the financial freedom you deserve.

Month 5: Building Your Emergency Fund and Beyond

'Do not save what is left after spending, but spend what is left after saving.'

—Warren Buffett

CONGRATULATIONS ON TAKING SIGNIFICANT STEPS TOWARDS FINANCIAL empowerment! By opening your bank account, tracking expenses, creating your personal financial statement, understanding cash flows, establishing a budget and identifying smart goals, you have laid a strong foundation for your financial journey. Now, it's time to build on that foundation by understanding the true importance of an emergency fund.

An emergency fund is like a financial safety net, a dedicated pool of money set aside to cover unforeseen and urgent expenses. It acts as a buffer, providing you with peace of mind during challenging times. Your emergency fund is not meant for big-ticket purchases or splurging on luxuries; its sole purpose is to shield you from financial stress during emergencies.

The Power of an Emergency Fund

Meet Sheetal, a single woman in her thirties working in the hospitality industry. Diligently, she built an emergency fund equivalent to six months of her living expenses. When the COVID-19 pandemic struck, her employer temporarily laid off staff, including Sheetal. Fortunately, with her emergency fund in place, Sheetal had the financial support she needed to cover her bills and living expenses during this tough period of unemployment. This fund allowed her to focus on searching for new job opportunities without having to worry about immediate financial concerns.

Similarly, Ranjan and Riya, who have two young children, always understood the importance of an emergency fund in their financial planning. When Riya unexpectedly lost her job due to company downsizing during the pandemic, they were grateful for their emergency fund. Instead of having to depend on Ranjan's income alone, the fund provided them with the breathing space to adjust their budget and focus on finding a new job for Riya without any panic or fear of financial instability. This reduced the pressure on Ranjan and prevented these financial concerns from straining their relation.

Building Your Emergency Fund

Now that you recognise the significance of an emergency fund, it's time to take actionable steps to build one for yourself.

Step 1: Set a target. Begin by calculating your monthly living expenses and aim to save at least three to six months' worth in your emergency fund. This amount will provide you with enough cushion to weather most unexpected financial storms.

Step 2: Automate savings. Make saving for your emergency fund a priority by setting up automatic transfers from your checking account to a dedicated savings account. Treating this as a non-negotiable expense will help you build your fund consistently.

Step 3: Keep it liquid and separate. Ensure your emergency fund is easily accessible, such as in a savings account or a money market account. Keep it separate from your regular savings and investment accounts to avoid any temptation to use it for non-emergencies.

Step 4: Replenish after use. If you ever need to tap into your emergency fund, make it a priority to replenish it as soon as you can. Aim to restore it to the recommended three to six months' worth of expenses to maintain your financial safety net.

Risk Management Beyond the Emergency Fund

Building an emergency fund lays a solid foundation for financial stability, but it's essential to consider broader risk management strategies to secure your financial future. This includes addressing health-related expenses and potential loss of income due to disability or death.

Health and Life Cover for Women

Medical emergencies can quickly drain savings or force the liquidation of assets. Health insurance transfers this financial risk to the provider, offering comprehensive coverage for a relatively small premium. This preserves hard-earned savings and investments, providing peace of mind amidst uncertainties.

For women who play a significant role in contributing to their family's income, health insurance is paramount. This serves as a vital safety net for managing medical expenses and ensuring that financial goals remain on track. Group health coverage, especially if provided through employment, can offer valuable benefits, often including coverage for pregnancy-related expenses.

Moreover, today, there is the possibility to transfer your group health cover to an individual policy if you plan to take a break or leave your current company. This option provides continuity of coverage and ensures ongoing protection, even amidst employment changes. It's advisable to inform your group insurance provider at least six months in advance to facilitate a smooth transition.

Supplementing your group health cover with an individual health insurance policy further enhances your financial security. This additional layer of protection ensures that you have comprehensive coverage tailored to your specific needs, safeguarding your health and financial well-being regardless of changes in employment status.

Adequate Term Insurance

Additionally, having sufficient term insurance is vital for financial security. It offers a lump sum amount to beneficiaries in the event of untimely demise, ensuring ongoing financial stability for loved ones. Avoiding mixed investment-insurance products simplifies coverage, focusing solely on providing financial protection.

Risk management is integral to financial resilience. While emergency funds provide immediate support, health and life cover shield against long-term financial impacts of unforeseen events. Prioritising health and securing adequate insurance safeguards against uncertainties, empowering individuals to navigate life's challenges with confidence and stability.

Contingency Funds, Risk Management, and SMART Life Automation Amidst Uncertainty

The COVID-19 pandemic underscores the importance of prudent financial management, particularly in maintaining emergency funds and managing money wisely. Real-life experiences highlight the significance of these practices:

1. *Loss of income*: Emergency funds cushioned the blow for many facing job loss or reduced income, providing temporary relief until stability was regained.
2. *Healthcare expenses*: Those with emergency funds weathered the surge in healthcare costs, avoiding crippling debt.
3. *Business closures*: Small business owners sustained operations through emergency funds, affording time to adapt to changing circumstances.
4. *Supply chain disruptions*: Emergency funds mitigated the impact of price hikes, maintaining financial stability amid market uncertainties.
5. *Travel cancellations*: Emergency funds eased the financial burden of cancelled plans, allowing flexibility in adapting to unforeseen circumstances.

In navigating financial uncertainties, the SMART Money Management Accounting System serves as a valuable tool, facilitating prudent money management and the accumulation of emergency funds.

Implementing a risk management strategy after establishing an emergency fund and before delving into investments, ensuring holistic financial resilience and security, is a necessary measure in your journey to becoming financially smart.

Month 6: Start Saving and Investing Towards Your Goals, Including Retirement

'The best time to plant a tree was twenty years ago. The second-best time is now.'

—Chinese Proverb

Congratulations on your continued journey toward financial empowerment! In this chapter, we will stress the importance of starting to save and investing in the right asset classes based on your goals, timeframe and risk appetite. Particularly for women, planning your investments well is essential, considering factors such as longer lifespans, earning disparities and career breaks for family and caregiving responsibilities.

Step 1: Define Your Goals and Bridge the Gap

The first step towards building a strong financial future is defining your goals and understanding how much you need to achieve them. Take some time to list your short-term and long-term goals, such as buying a house, funding your children's education or retiring comfortably. Having a clear understanding of your financial objectives will guide your investment decisions.

By understanding the gap between your current financial standing and your desired future outcomes, you can develop a strategic plan to bridge that divide. Whether it involves saving diligently, investing prudently or seeking additional sources of income, defining your goals empowers you to take proactive steps towards realising your dreams.

Step 2: Choose the Right Investment Plan

With your goals clearly defined, the next pivotal step is selecting the appropriate investment plan to propel you towards achieving them. Recognise that each goal may encompass varying timeframes and risk tolerances, necessitating a tailored investment strategy for each objective.

Exercise caution against the allure of schemes promising lofty returns with minimal risk. Instead, prioritise reliability and prudence in your investment choices. Opt for established and reputable investment vehicles that align with your risk profile and time horizon.

Diversification is key to mitigating risk and optimising returns across your investment portfolio. Consider allocating assets across a spectrum of investment options, including stocks, bonds, mutual funds and real estate, to spread risk and capture growth opportunities.

By making informed decisions and staying committed to your investment strategy, you lay the groundwork for financial success and the realization of your aspirations.

Step 3: Invest in Long-Term Instruments—Mutual Funds

For long-term financial goals extending beyond five years, harnessing the potential of mutual funds can be a game-changing strategy. Mutual funds offer a diversified and professionally managed approach to investing, making them an ideal choice for accumulating wealth over extended periods.

A mutual fund aggregates capital from numerous investors sharing a common investment objective and allocates it across a diverse range of asset classes, including equities and bonds. This diversification helps spread risk and optimise returns over the long haul.

Equity mutual funds, in particular, have a proven track record of delivering attractive returns over the long term, averaging around 12% annually. This makes them an appealing option for investors seeking substantial growth opportunities for their long-term financial objectives.

Whether you opt for a lump sum investment or choose to invest systematically through a systematic investment plan (SIP), mutual funds offer flexibility and accessibility to suit your investment preferences. SIPs, in particular, enable you to invest small, regular amounts at predetermined intervals, helping to instil financial discipline and capitalise on market fluctuations through rupee-cost averaging.

By leveraging the power of mutual funds for your long-term goals, you position yourself to potentially benefit from the growth potential of the equity market while mitigating risk through diversification. With prudent investment decisions and a steadfast commitment to your financial plan, mutual funds can serve as a cornerstone in building wealth and realising your aspirations in the long run.

Step 4: Park Your Short-Term Funds Wisely

Safeguarding your short-term funds is paramount for financial security and flexibility. Whether earmarked for imminent goals or emergency reserves, liquidity and safety are essential. Explore options that offer accessibility and stability to ensure your funds remain readily available when needed.

Consider allocating your short-term funds to liquid mutual funds or fixed deposits, which strike a balance between accessibility and security. Liquid mutual funds provide easy access to your funds while potentially offering higher returns compared to traditional savings accounts. These funds typically invest in short-term, high-quality debt instruments, making them relatively safe investments.

Similarly, fixed deposits offer a stable return on your investment over a predetermined period, providing a predictable source of income. By parking your short-term funds in these avenues, you can mitigate risk while earning a modest return on your investment.

Returns on these short-term instruments typically range from 3–6%, contingent on the duration of the investment and prevailing market conditions. This prudent approach ensures that your funds remain readily available for emergencies or future financial needs, offering both security and the potential for incremental growth.

By wisely parking your short-term funds in instruments with liquidity and safety, you fortify your financial foundation and maintain the flexibility to navigate unforeseen circumstances with confidence and ease.

Step 5: Beware of Ponzi Schemes and Chit Funds

To safeguard your financial well-being, you must stay vigilant and avoid Ponzi schemes or chit funds that promise unrealistic returns. These fraudulent schemes pose significant risks and can result in substantial financial losses.

In a Ponzi scheme, returns are paid to existing investors using the capital contributed by new investors, rather than from profits generated by the underlying business. The scheme collapses when there are not enough new investors to sustain the payouts, leading to investors losing a lot of money.

To mitigate the risk of falling victim to such schemes, educate yourself about the warning signs and red flags associated with fraudulent investments. Be wary of schemes that promise exceptionally high returns with minimal risk, as they often carry elevated levels of risk and are unsustainable in the long term.

Instead, focus on learning more about reputable investment options, such as mutual funds, through credible sources. Mutual funds offer a diversified and professionally managed approach to investing, making them suitable for investors seeking long-term growth opportunities while minimising risk.

Informed decision-making and thorough research before investing can help you protect yourself from fraudulent schemes. Remember to align your investments with your financial goals, timeframe and risk tolerance, and seek advice from trusted financial professionals if needed.

By adopting a prudent approach to saving and investing, you can pave the way for a financially secure and prosperous future while avoiding the pitfalls of fraudulent schemes. Investing in mutual funds for long-term goals and maintaining stability with liquid funds and fixed deposits for short-term needs can help you achieve your financial objectives with confidence and peace of mind.

Some Real-Life Cases

Sunita was able to use the power of saving to pay for her daughter's college education without any financial stress.

Sunita's journey exemplifies the power of foresight, discipline and strategic financial planning in securing her daughter's college education without financial strain. From the moment her daughter was born, Sunita saved a portion of her income each month. She understood that the cost of education would only rise over time and took proactive steps to start saving early.

As her daughter grew older, Sunita continued to diligently save and diversified her investment portfolio by allocating some of her savings into mutual funds. This decision proved fruitful, as it offered her a better return on investment compared to a traditional savings account. By harnessing the potential for higher returns through mutual funds, Sunita accelerated her journey towards her financial goal.

By the time her daughter reached high school, Sunita realised that her savings, bolstered by investments in mutual funds, had accumulated to a level where she could comfortably finance her daughter's college education. She didn't need to take out loans or burden her daughter with student debt.

Sunita's prudent financial decisions also extended to leveraging government schemes announced especially for the girl child, such as the Sukanya Samriddhi Yojana, which provided attractive interest rates and tax benefits. Sunita further optimised her savings strategy by using such schemes, maximising the resources available to her.

Ultimately, Sunita's unwavering commitment to saving, investing and staying informed about financial opportunities enabled her to fulfil her aspiration of providing the best education for her daughter. Her story serves as an inspiring testament to the transformative impact of disciplined financial planning in achieving long-term goals and securing a brighter future for loved ones.

Leena benefited from long-term investing and diversifying her portfolio.

Leena is a financially smart woman who started investing in long-term equity mutual funds in her twenties. She understood the importance of investing early and regularly, which allowed her to accumulate wealth over time.

Leena was also aware of the risks involved in equity investments, but she knew that over the long term, equity investments tend to give better returns than other investments. So, she continued to invest small amounts regularly over the years, even when the market was down, which averaged out her investments and reduced risks.

As the years passed, Leena's investments grew, and she diversified her investments by creating a portfolio of different equity mutual funds. She also ensured that her asset allocation was balanced and aligned with her long-term financial goals.

By the time Leena retired, her investments had grown significantly, and she was able to retire comfortably without any financial stress. Her disciplined approach to investing over the years paid off, and she was able to enjoy the benefits of her investments.

Leena's example demonstrates the importance of starting to invest early, diversifying investments and having a disciplined approach to investing. These steps can help in building wealth over the long term, which can be beneficial in achieving long-term financial goals and retiring comfortably without any financial stress.

Ria made a smart financial move by investing in SIPs.

Ria's smart financial move of investing in mutual funds through a systematic investment plan (SIP) exemplifies the power of disciplined investing and the benefits of compounding returns. By committing to invest a fixed amount at regular intervals, Ria ensured a consistent approach to building her investment portfolio.

Through SIPs, Ria capitalised on the principle of compounding, where her investments generated returns not only on her initial investment but also on the accumulated earnings. This compounding effect led to significant growth in her investment portfolio over time.

Even during a career break to focus on raising her children, Ria's investments continued to work for her, generating returns and providing her with financial stability without the need for additional contributions. This highlights the resilience and passive income potential of well-structured investment plans.

Ria's story underscores the importance of starting early and investing consistently to reap the benefits of compounding. It demonstrates how even modest investments made over an extended period can result in substantial returns, paving the way for financial security and peace of mind.

Selecting the right mutual funds tailored to one's financial goals, risk tolerance and investment horizon is also key. By making informed decisions and staying committed to their investment journey, individuals like Ria can secure their financial future and achieve their long-term financial objectives.

> ### Action Points
>
> 1. Define your financial goals and calculate how much you need to achieve them.
> 2. Identify the right investment plan tailored to your goals and risk tolerance.
> 3. Consider investing in long-term mutual funds for higher returns.
> 4. Park your short-term funds in liquid mutual funds or fixed deposits for easy access.
> 5. Stay informed and avoid Ponzi schemes and chit funds.
> 6. Look out for mutual fund courses to enhance your understanding of mutual funds and make informed investment choices.

Month 7: Review Your Progress and Make Necessary Changes

'Continuous improvement is better than delayed perfection.'
—Mark Twain

CONGRATULATIONS ON REACHING THE FINAL MONTH OF OUR SEVEN-month action plan to take control of your financial life! By now, you've made significant strides towards financial empowerment. However, remember that the journey to financial freedom is an ongoing process that requires continuous effort and dedication.

In this chapter, we will focus on reviewing your progress, making necessary adjustments and embracing continuous learning to ensure your financial success.

Celebrate your accomplishments, no matter how big or small, and acknowledge the challenges you've faced along the way. Reflecting on your journey allows you to appreciate how far you've come and identify any lessons learned that can guide your future financial decisions.

Step 1: Schedule a Money Date with Yourself

As you embark on this month, set aside a few hours for a 'money date' with yourself. Find a comfortable and distraction-free environment, whether it's at home with your laptop or notebook, or at your favourite café. This dedicated time allows you to focus solely on your financial review.

During your money date, immerse yourself in a comprehensive review of your financial journey over the past six months. Delve into the data you've diligently tracked—your cash flows, expenses and savings. Take note of any trends or patterns that have emerged, both positive and negative.

Reflect on whether you've adhered to your budget across all segments of your finances. Identify areas where you may have exceeded your budget or where unexpected expenses arose. Conversely, celebrate the areas where you've successfully maintained or even surpassed your financial targets.

Assess your ability to accurately predict your money flows. Consider whether your initial budget projections aligned with your actual income and expenses. Analyse any discrepancies and explore the underlying factors contributing to these variations.

Based on your observations, identify areas for improvement and set actionable goals for the future. Consider what adjustments you can make to enhance your financial management practices and ensure greater alignment with your long-term objectives. Whether it's refining your budgeting strategies, exploring new avenues for saving or investing or seeking ways to increase your income, adopt initiatives that will propel you closer to financial success.

Celebrate the progress you've made thus far as well as your achievements and milestones. Acknowledge the dedication and effort you've invested in your financial journey and take pride in the steps you've taken towards building a more secure financial future.

Ultimately, remember that your money date is not just a routine review—it's an opportunity for empowerment and growth. By engaging in this reflective process, you equip yourself with the insights and awareness needed to make informed decisions that positively impact your financial well-being.

Step 2: Review Your Investment Portfolio

Now is the perfect time to conduct a thorough review of your investment portfolio to ensure it remains aligned with your financial objectives. Begin by assessing the performance of your investments and evaluating whether they are meeting your expectations.

Scrutinise each component of your portfolio and analyse its performance relative to relevant benchmarks and your established goals. Identify any assets that may be underperforming or exhibiting signs of volatility. Conversely, celebrate the successes of investments that have exceeded expectations and contributed positively to your overall portfolio growth.

Consider the importance of diversification in managing risk and optimising returns. Assess the diversification of your portfolio across different asset classes, industries and geographic regions. Determine whether adjustments are necessary to rebalance your portfolio and mitigate concentration risk.

Seek professional advice if you're uncertain about specific investment decisions or require assistance in optimising your portfolio. A financial advisor can provide valuable insights and guidance tailored to your unique circumstances and objectives.

Remember that your investment strategy should always reflect your risk tolerance, time horizon and financial goals. As such, periodically reviewing and adjusting your portfolio ensures that it remains well-suited to support your long-term financial aspirations.

By dedicating time to review your investment portfolio, you empower yourself to make informed decisions that enhance the performance and resilience of your investment holdings. Stay proactive and vigilant in managing your investments to maximise their potential and safeguard your financial future.

Step 3: Seek Guidance from a Qualified Financial Coach or Mentor

Embarking on a financial journey can be daunting, especially without proper guidance and support. Consider enlisting the assistance of a qualified financial coach or mentor to provide insights and guidance.

A financial coach or mentor possesses the expertise and experience to help you navigate various financial challenges and opportunities. Whether you're striving to achieve specific financial goals, create a comprehensive financial plan or make informed investment decisions, a knowledgeable mentor can offer advice tailored to you.

When selecting a financial coach or mentor, examine their qualifications, credentials and relevant experience. Look for individuals with a proven record of success in financial coaching or mentoring, as well as a deep understanding of personal finance principles and strategies.

Engaging with a financial coach or mentor offers several benefits, including:

1. *Goal clarity*: A skilled mentor can assist you in clarifying your financial goals and developing a structured plan to achieve them. By aligning your objectives with actionable steps, you can make meaningful progress towards financial success.

2. *Accountability*: Having a mentor provides built-in accountability, encouraging you to stay committed to your financial objectives and follow through on your action plan. Regular check-ins and progress assessments ensure that you remain on track towards your goals.

3. *Expert guidance*: A coach or mentor can offer expert guidance on a wide range of financial topics, including budgeting, saving, investing, debt management and retirement planning. Their insights can help you make informed decisions and avoid common pitfalls.

4. *Emotional support*: Navigating financial challenges can be emotionally taxing, but a supportive mentor can offer encouragement, motivation and perspective during difficult times. Their guidance can instil confidence and resilience as you work towards financial empowerment.

5. *Lifelong learning*: Working with a mentor provides opportunities for continuous learning and skill development in personal finance. By leveraging their expertise and insights, you can expand your financial knowledge and improve your financial literacy over time.

Whether you're just beginning your financial journey or seeking to refine your existing strategies, partnering with a qualified financial coach or mentor can accelerate your progress and enhance your financial well-being. Invest in your financial future by taking this step.

Step 4: Time Block for Financial Goals

Creating dedicated time blocks in your calendar for working on your financial goals is a powerful strategy for realising your objectives and staying focused on achieving them. These time blocks should be frequent enough to ensure consistent progress, typically occurring at least once or twice a week, depending on your schedule and the complexity of your financial goals.

When scheduling these time blocks, consider allocating anywhere from 30 minutes to a few hours, depending on the tasks you need to accomplish and the depth of analysis required. Shorter time blocks can be used for routine financial tasks such as reviewing expenses, tracking savings progress or updating your budget. Longer time blocks may be necessary for more in-depth activities such as researching investment opportunities conducting portfolio reviews or developing a comprehensive financial plan.

During these time blocks, focus on a variety of financial activities, including:

1. *Reviewing financial statements*: Take time to review your bank statements, credit card statements and investment account statements. Check for any discrepancies, unauthorised transactions or opportunities to optimise your spending and saving habits.
2. *Updating budgets and financial plans*: Review your budget and financial plan regularly to ensure they align with your current financial situation and goals. Make any necessary adjustments to accommodate changes in income, expenses or priorities.
3. *Researching investment opportunities*: If you're considering new investment opportunities or strategies, use your time

blocks to conduct thorough research. Explore different asset classes, investment vehicles and market trends to make informed decisions.

4. *Setting and monitoring goals*: Use your time blocks to set specific, measurable financial goals and track your progress towards achieving them. Break down larger goals into smaller, actionable steps and celebrate milestones along the way.

5. *Educating yourself*: Dedicate time to ongoing financial education and skill development. Read books and articles or attend webinars on relevant personal finance topics.

6. *Seeking professional advice*: If you have complex financial needs or questions, consider using your time blocks to consult with a qualified financial advisor or coach. Use this opportunity to ask questions, seek guidance and gain clarity on important financial matters.

By time-blocking for your financial goals, you establish a structured approach to managing your finances and ensure that they receive the attention they deserve. Treat these time blocks as non-negotiable commitments to your financial well-being and use them to make meaningful progress towards your financial objectives.

Step 5: Stay Focused on What Matters

Identify the key actions that will have the most significant impact on achieving your financial goals. Whether it's increasing your savings rate, reducing debt or investing, prioritise the activities that align most closely with your objectives.

Stay committed to these essential actions and avoid getting distracted by less critical tasks. It's easy to become overwhelmed by the multitude of financial responsibilities and decisions we face daily. By staying focused on what truly matters, you can allocate your time and resources more effectively.

Eliminate unnecessary financial commitments and focus on the strategies that will propel you towards your objectives. This may involve reassessing your spending habits, cutting back on non-essential expenses or renegotiating existing contracts and subscriptions. By streamlining your financial commitments, you free up resources to allocate towards your highest priorities.

Remember, staying focused on what matters requires discipline and consistency. Regularly review your progress, adjust your strategies as needed and remain committed to your long-term vision. By prioritising the actions that have the greatest impact on your financial well-being, you set yourself up for success.

Step 6: Embrace Continuous Learning

Work towards educating yourself about personal finance and investment strategies continuously. Read books, attend financial workshops or seminars and seek information from reputable sources. Continuous learning not only enhances your financial knowledge but also empowers you to make more strategic and confident decisions. It allows you to stay ahead of market developments, understand complex financial concepts and identify new opportunities for growth.

Ongoing education helps you navigate financial challenges and uncertainties with resilience and agility. Whether it's learning about new investment vehicles, understanding tax implications or exploring advanced financial planning techniques, every bit of knowledge gained contributes to your financial well-being.

Personal finance is a dynamic field, and there's always something new to learn. Continuous learning ensures that you remain well-informed and adaptable in managing your finances, ultimately leading to greater financial success and security.

Step 7: Celebrate Your Progress

Don't forget to celebrate your progress along the way! Take the time to acknowledge the small victories you have achieved on your financial journey and treat yourself to a small reward for your hard work and dedication.

Celebrating milestones, no matter how minor, helps maintain motivation and momentum towards your financial goals. It reinforces the progress you've made and reminds you of the positive impact of your efforts.

Do something enjoyable or indulge in a treat that brings you joy. Whether it's a special dinner, a leisure activity you love or even a simple moment of relaxation, find ways to mark your accomplishments and express gratitude for your financial growth.

Remember that each step forward, no matter how small, contributes to your overall success. By celebrating your progress, you reinforce your commitment to financial well-being and cultivate a positive mindset that fuels continued progress in the future.

Taking charge of your financial life is indeed a transformative journey that demands dedication, self-reflection and ongoing growth. By following these steps—reviewing progress, making necessary adjustments, seeking guidance, time-blocking for goals, staying focused, embracing learning and celebrating achievements—you're laying the foundation for a financially prosperous and fulfilling life.

But remember, financial empowerment isn't a one-time achievement; it's a lifelong pursuit. As you move forward beyond this action plan, stay committed to your goals, keep educating yourself and remain proactive in managing your finances. With persistence and resilience, you can create the life you desire and achieve long-term financial well-being.

Case Study: Meera's Journey to Financial Empowerment

Meera, a forty-year-old widow, found herself facing the daunting task of securing her and her son Anand's financial future after her husband's untimely demise. Seeking guidance, she reached out to us as we specialise in financial planning for women.

Initial Assessment: During our first meeting, Meera revealed that her primary income source was the interest earned from a fixed deposit of ₹15 lakhs, received from her husband's life insurance policy. Her monthly expenses were ₹8,000, and she had a modest salary of ₹10,000 from her job as an assistant.

Identifying Gaps: Meera lacked emergency savings, health insurance and life insurance cover. Recognising these gaps in Meera's financial situation, we outlined a plan to address them comprehensively. Together, we embarked on a journey to build financial security and stability for Meera and Anand.

Financial Planning Strategies:

1. *Emergency fund creation:* We recommended creating an emergency fund equivalent to six to nine months of expenses. Meera was advised to reallocate a portion of her fixed deposit into liquid and debt mutual funds to ensure accessibility in case of unexpected expenses.
2. *Insurance coverage:* Meera obtained a family floater health insurance policy and adequate term insurance

coverage to safeguard against medical emergencies and income loss.

3. *Goal setting and investment planning:* Clear financial goals were established for Anand's education and Meera's retirement. Mutual funds were chosen as the investment vehicle, offering safety and growth potential. Meera initiated systematic investment plans (SIPs) to systematically save and invest for the future.

4. *Budgeting and financial discipline:* Meera learnt the importance of budgeting and prioritising financial goals. She committed to disciplined saving and investing, supplemented by additional income from tailoring assignments.

5. *Continuous Monitoring and Review:* Regular progress reviews enabled Meera to track her financial journey and make necessary adjustments. This ongoing monitoring ensured that she remained focused on her goals and maintained financial discipline.

6. *Outcome:* Today, Meera stands as a financially empowered woman, equipped with the knowledge and tools to navigate her financial future confidently. Through her dedication and commitment, she not only secured her own financial well-being but also inspires others to embark on their own journeys to financial empowerment.

7. *Key Lessons Learnt:* Meera's case highlights the importance of seeking professional financial guidance, setting clear goals and maintaining discipline in financial planning. By addressing gaps, setting goals and adhering to a structured financial plan, Meera achieved financial security and peace of mind for herself and her son. Her journey serves as a testament to the transformative power of financial planning in shaping one's future.

Action Points

1. Schedule a money date with yourself to review your progress.
2. Evaluate your investment portfolio and consider diversification.
3. Seek guidance from a qualified financial coach or mentor.
4. Time block specific intervals for working on your financial goals.
5. Stay focused on the key actions that matter most in achieving your goals.
6. Continue learning about personal finance and investment strategies.
7. Celebrate your progress and small victories along the way.

Section 5

Mastering Financial Resilience and Empowerment

'Financial peace isn't the acquisition of stuff. It's learning to live on less than you make, so you can give money back and have money to invest. You can't win until you do this.'

—Dave Ramsey

In this section, we delve into the intricate world of financial resilience and mastery. Just as a well-built fortress withstands the test of time, your financial foundation demands a comprehensive shield against potential risks, a calculated strategy for investments and a plan to secure your legacy.

From safeguarding your health and life to understanding the dynamic landscape of investments, this section is designed to empower you with the knowledge and tools you need to confidently navigate the complexities of modern finances. We will uncover the art of risk management, decode the fundamentals of investment and shed light on the crucial aspects of securing your financial future.

We will also delve into the significance of crafting a legacy that echoes your values and ensures the prosperity of your loved ones. We'll equip you with the insights needed to navigate challenges on your journey successfully.

So, let us embark on this journey together, as we unveil the secrets to mastering financial resilience and empowerment.

Safeguarding Your Financial Foundation with Health Coverage

'Good health is not something we can buy. However, it can be an extremely valuable savings account.'
—Anne Wilson Schaef

WHILE WE PLAN FOR THE FUTURE, HEALTH EMERGENCIES CAN THROW us off balance. This chapter explores how health coverage is like a safety net, protecting us from financial chaos during tough times. Through relatable stories and practical advice, we'll uncover why health insurance matters and how to choose the right one for you and your family.

Ishita, a single mother had dedicated to providing the best life for her daughter, Aanya. Ishita's world turned upside down when she fell critically ill, facing the daunting prospect of extensive medical treatment as she was detected with breast cancer. The looming financial burden of medical expenses added another layer of worry. With bills mounting and her savings dwindling, Ishita felt her dream of securing a bright future for Aanya slipping away.

Yet, Ishita wasn't alone in her plight. Years prior, she had made an important decision to invest in a comprehensive health insurance policy. Having paid the premiums for five years in a row without making a single claim, Ishita began to question the necessity of continuing payments, viewing it merely as an expense. However, her insurance agent urged her to continue the policy, emphasising its role as a vital risk management tool and a potential lifesaver.

Little did she know that this decision would prove to be her saving grace. As she found herself admitted to the hospital for treatment, the true worth of her health insurance policy became clear. It wasn't just a document; it was a lifeline that offered a beacon of hope. All her expenses while in the hospital were taken care of, and she didn't need to dip into her savings anymore.

She realised how different her situation would have been without the foresight to secure adequate health coverage. Knowing her medical expenses were covered gave her peace of mind and allowed her to prioritise her health.

Ishita's health insurance policy protected not only her health but also her financial stability. It ensured that her dreams for Aanya were not shattered by unforeseen medical costs. Ishita's story highlights that health coverage is not just an expense— it's an investment in our well-being and the well-being of our loved ones.

Her journey underscores the profound impact that health insurance can have on our lives. Its power lies in shielding us from the financial turmoil that often accompanies medical emergencies. Her story serves as a powerful reminder that securing our health also means not just securing our financial future but also that of our loved ones.

Risk Management through Health Insurance

Imagine yourself or a loved one requiring major medical intervention. In such situations, expenses can quickly spiral out of control, and without proper planning, the financial aftermath can be overwhelming. Many individuals resort to using their savings or fixed deposits, or even liquidate investments at inopportune times, possibly incurring losses, just to have access to enough liquid funds. There have been cases where even the sale of valuable assets like gold or property becomes a necessity, or loans are taken out to cover medical bills. Health is indeed wealth, and ensuring proper funding for medical expenses is a priority.

Instead of depleting your hard-earned savings or investments, one smart approach is to transfer the risk to someone else by paying a relatively small premium. This is where health insurance comes into play. By purchasing a health insurance policy, you effectively transfer the financial risk of medical emergencies to the insurance provider. This means that for the cost of the amount you pay as premium, you gain access to a much larger coverage, safeguarding you from the devastating impact of unforeseen medical expenses.

Let's break it down with an example: Suppose you opt for a health insurance policy with a coverage of 10 lakhs. If you encounter a hospital bill of 3 lakhs, you should be eligible for a refund of 3 lakhs from the policy. This not only eases the financial burden but also allows you to maintain your savings and investments for other important life goals.

While life insurance is crucial, health coverage holds unique importance. We are more likely to require medical treatment due to accidents, illnesses or surgeries than to pass away suddenly. Furthermore, the probability of living longer is higher than an early demise. Relying on others during your health crisis is not an option you'd want to entertain. That's why, if you have to choose between health insurance and life insurance, it's best if you take health insurance first.

However, choosing the right health insurance policy isn't as straightforward as it might seem. With over forty companies offering a variety of plans, each with numerous features and options, the task can be overwhelming. While comparison websites can be helpful, a qualified mentor or coach can provide personalised guidance tailored to your specific requirements.

Health coverage is a cornerstone of financial preparedness. The power of health insurance lies in its ability to safeguard your savings, investments and overall financial well-being during unforeseen medical emergencies. A good health insurance policy ensures that you can confidently tackle health challenges without compromising your financial future.

Health insurance is a must for everyone. Most companies cover their employees via group health insurance and that's where many employees keep postponing taking up an individual health cover as they feel they are already covered under the employer's group cover.

Employer Coverage vs Individual Cover—Making the Right Choice

It's a common query—should we rely solely on our employer's coverage or buy an individual health insurance as well?

In addition to the group cover, having an individual policy always helps. Let's unravel this aspect further and understand why having your own individual health insurance policy is paramount, even if you're already covered by your employer.

Picture this scenario: Sarita and Sudhir, a couple leading a comfortable life, were covered by their respective employer's health insurance policies. With an impressive group coverage of 25 lakhs each, they felt adequately protected. However, Sudhir was laid off during the COVID-19 pandemic. Suddenly, the reassuring safety net provided by his employer's health insurance vanished, leaving their family vulnerable to unforeseen medical expenses. It was a stark reminder that relying solely on employer coverage can leave crucial gaps in one's financial safety net.

Fortunately, there are options available now to bridge this gap. According to health insurance rules, individuals covered under any group health insurance policy have the right to migrate to an individual health insurance policy or a family floater policy with the same insurer. This means that even after leaving their job, Sarita and Sudhir could transfer their benefits to an individual policy, thereby ensuring continued coverage for themselves and their family.

Understanding the Process of Migration

A group health insurance policy typically covers employees and sometimes their family members, with the premium paid by the employer. However, when the employee leaves the organization, the cover ceases to exist. To migrate from a group cover to an individual or family floater health insurance plan of the same insurer, you need to intimate the group insurance company well in advance, preferably at least thirty days prior to the last employment date.

To initiate the migration process, individuals must provide certain documents to the insurer, including a proposal form, portability form, and a copy of the resignation or retirement letter. The insurer may also require additional information before issuing a new policy.

Key Advantages of Migration

One of the significant advantages of migrating from a group cover is that you are given credit for the number of years of continuous insurance coverage. This means that waiting periods, including those for pre-existing diseases, are considered based on the time spent under the group policy.

While migrating to an individual policy, you are liable to share the details of potential health concerns, and there is a possibility of fresh medical underwriting. The premium for the individual policy will depend on the new insurer's underwriting of the policy.

Even though migration is allowed, there could be health concerns, and fresh medical underwriting may pose problems. Therefore, it's advisable to consider migrating to ensure continued coverage and financial security. Once migrated, individuals should ensure that the policy document carries the credit of waiting periods from the group cover.

Additionally, they may choose to port to a different insurer anytime around forty-five days before the next renewal date for added flexibility.

Steps for a Smooth Migration

1. *Intimate your insurer early:* Notify your group insurance company about your intent to migrate at least thirty days before your last employment date.

2. *Gather necessary documents:* Prepare and submit the proposal form, portability form and a copy of your resignation or retirement letter.

3. *Check waiting period credits:* Ensure that your new policy document reflects the credit for the years of continuous coverage from your group policy, especially for pre-existing diseases.

4. *Be ready for medical underwriting:* Be prepared to disclose health concerns and potentially undergo fresh medical underwriting. The premium for the new individual policy will depend on this assessment.

5. *Consider portability for flexibility:* After migration, you can opt to port your policy to a different insurer around forty-five days before the next renewal date if needed.

Health insurance migration is a crucial step in maintaining continuous and reliable coverage, especially when transitioning between jobs or during employment gaps. For Sarita and Sudhir, and many others like them, understanding and utilizing these migration options ensures that their financial safety net remains intact, providing peace of mind and security for themselves and their families. This knowledge not only empowers you to secure your health coverage but also equips you to navigate the complexities of health insurance with confidence.

Uncle Harish and Aunt Sonal's Journey

This is a gripping tale of resilience in the face of unforeseen challenges. Uncle Harish was a long-time employee of a multinational company, while Aunt Sonal was a retired bank employee. Both were now aged above seventy-five and were leading a comfortable retired life. They did not buy any individual health covers as Uncle's company had extended the group health cover even post-retirement for the employee and his entire family. For years, they trusted that this coverage would be their safety net, shielding them from any medical emergencies that might arise. So, they invested their money, but did not invest in a health insurance policy and did not have a risk management plan

However, fate had other plans in store for them. When the company underwent a change in ownership, Uncle Harish and Aunt Sonal were met with a harsh reality. The health insurance coverage they had come to rely on was suddenly discontinued for retired employees. Aunt Sonal had a meagre 3 lakh cover from her bank. Overnight, their sense of security was shattered, leaving them exposed and vulnerable.

The true test of their resilience came when Uncle Harish fell into a coma, requiring urgent and extensive medical treatment and was on ventilator support for months. The family had to keep a 24-hour nurse, and after three months of hospitalisation, Uncle was recommended a home ICU facility. The sudden loss of their health coverage added an overwhelming layer of stress to an already dire situation. With medical bills mounting and little insurance to ease the burden, Aunt Sonal found herself facing one of the toughest challenges of her life.

Amidst the turmoil, Aunt Sonal had the daunting responsibility of securing individual health insurance for herself. However, this seemingly straightforward task proved to be anything but easy. The premiums for individual coverage at her age were exorbitant, far beyond what they could afford, and Aunt Sonal's preexisting medical conditions only exacerbated the difficulty. Finally, they had to dip into their retirement kitty, sell a real estate property in distress and redeem their investments to take care of the medical expenses.

Their journey is a poignant reminder of the importance of proactive planning and the limitations of relying solely on employer-provided health insurance. Despite their years of dedication and service, Uncle Harish and Aunt Sonal found themselves ill-prepared to face medical emergencies without adequate insurance coverage.

Their story serves as a sobering lesson for us all, prompting us to carefully assess our insurance needs and take proactive steps to protect ourselves and our loved ones.

Individual health insurance coverage holds immense significance for several reasons:

1. *Comprehensive protection*: Employer coverage may not always provide comprehensive protection for all family members. Individual policies allow you to customise coverage according to your family's specific needs, ensuring that everyone is adequately protected.
2. *Job changes and uncertainty*: The job market is unpredictable, and changes such as job loss or company transitions can leave you without health coverage. Your individual policy acts as a financial cushion during uncertain times, ensuring continuity of coverage regardless of your job status.
3. *Continuous coverage*: Individual health insurance remains with you throughout various life stages, including job changes, sabbaticals and retirement. It offers peace of mind knowing that you're covered even during transitions in employment or life circumstances.
4. *Customisation*: Individual policies allow for customisation based on your unique requirements. You have the flexibility

to choose the sum assured, add riders and tailor coverage to suit your family's needs.

The stories of Sarita, Sudhir, Uncle Harish and Aunt Sonal underscore the necessity of individual health insurance. While employer coverage is valuable, it has limitations and vulnerabilities. By securing personal health insurance, you not only protect your health but also safeguard your financial well-being and that of your loved ones.

Determining Your Health Cover Amount

Let me introduce you to Rajesh, a 35-year-old self-employed professional who believed in his invincibility and his ability to conquer any challenge that life threw at him. However, fate had a different plan, and Rajesh's journey would become a powerful lesson in the importance of comprehensive health coverage.

Being self-employed, Rajesh enjoyed the freedom of being his own boss. He revelled in the independence that came with his chosen career path, but he was also acutely aware of the uncertainties that came with self-employment. He didn't have the comfort of an employee group health insurance policy, so he had to take on the responsibility of ensuring his health and financial well-being.

One fateful day, Rajesh's life took an unexpected turn. While working late into the night, he experienced a sudden and intense bout of chest pain. Panic set in as he struggled to catch his breath, and his immediate instinct was to seek medical help. Rajesh was rushed to a well-known hospital in town, where he underwent a battery of tests and evaluations.

The diagnosis was a crushing blow—Rajesh was suffering from a severe cardiac condition that required immediate surgical intervention. As he grappled with the shock of his diagnosis, a new reality set in—the reality of mounting medical bills. The surgical procedures, hospitalisation expenses, medications and ongoing treatments began to accumulate rapidly.

Rajesh had opted for a health insurance policy with a coverage limit of ₹3 lakhs. At the time, he believed this amount would suffice for any medical emergencies that might arise. However, as his hospital stay extended and the costs mounted, Rajesh's confidence in his choice began to waver. The hospital he was admitted to was renowned for its advanced medical facilities, but it also came with significant expenses that his policy could not fully cover.

As Rajesh faced the daunting prospect of both a health crisis and a financial one, he wished he had chosen a more comprehensive health insurance policy. He understood the value of having coverage that could not only manage his medical expenses but also provide him with the peace of mind he needed during this challenging period.

Rajesh's experience underscores the importance of adequate health insurance coverage for self-employed individuals and a reminder that those without employer-provided group coverage must take proactive steps to protect their well-being and financial stability. Health insurance is not a mere formality; it is a lifeline that safeguards us from unforeseen circumstances. Investing wisely in comprehensive health coverage can provide financial protection and peace of mind during times of crisis.

Here's a breakdown of the key factors and thumb rules to consider when selecting your health insurance coverage:

1. *Geographical location and healthcare facilities*: Evaluate the average medical expenses in your locality, considering the varying costs of treatments and hospitalisation. Urban centres may offer advanced healthcare facilities but at higher prices. Choose a cover that aligns with the healthcare costs of your area.

2. *Preferred hospitals and privacy concerns*: Your choice of hospital significantly impacts your health cover amount. Opting for top-tier hospitals or private facilities may result in higher expenses. Consider any privacy concerns, such as the preference for private rooms, which come with additional costs.

3. *Age and healthcare costs*: Healthcare costs tend to escalate with age. Initiating your health insurance early allows you to benefit from lower premiums and accumulate no-claim bonuses over time.

4. *Balancing immediate needs and future protection*: Anticipate medical inflation and evolving healthcare needs when selecting your health cover amount. While a basic cover may seem sufficient now, choose comprehensive coverage for future needs.

Thumb Rules for Selecting the Right Health Insurance

- *Start early*: Initiate your health coverage as soon as possible to benefit from lower premiums.
- *Analyse healthcare costs*: Evaluate average medical expenses in your area to determine an appropriate coverage amount.

> - *Consider hospital preferences*: Factor in preferences for hospitals and room types, as they impact overall costs.
> - *Family-friendly coverage*: Opt for a floater policy covering all family members under a single sum insured for comprehensive coverage.
> - *Account for inflation*: Anticipate medical inflation and evolving healthcare needs to ensure your coverage offers protection against rising costs.

By selecting comprehensive coverage and starting your health insurance journey early, you can secure both your well-being and financial stability in the face of unforeseen medical expenses.

How to Select the Right Policy

Navigating the maze of health insurance policies can be daunting, but with the right approach, you can make informed decisions that safeguard your financial well-being. Here's how to choose the right health insurance policy:

1. *Decoding complexity with expert guidance*: The world of health insurance is vast and intricate. Seek the counsel of a financial coach or mentor who can help you understand the nuances of different policies and guide you towards the most suitable option for your needs.

2. *Research, research, research*: Thoroughly research insurance companies before deciding. Look into their reputation, management, network of hospitals and the efficiency of their third-party administrators (TPAs). TPAs play a crucial role in claims management, so their effectiveness is key.

3. *Understanding co-pay*: Be aware of co-pay, which is an arrangement through which you agree to bear a percentage of medical expenses. Understand how much of the payment will be made by the insurance provider and under what circumstances co-pay affects your finances during a medical emergency to avoid unexpected financial burdens.

4. *Debunking insurance ratings*: While insurance ratings can provide insights, approach them with caution. Conflicts of interest may compromise their accuracy. Use ratings as a starting point, but don't rely solely on them for decision-making.

5. *Using the three-part decision metric*: Assess policies based on price, benefits and claims. Consider whether the policy offers value for money, aligns with your medical needs and has a reliable claim settlement process. A policy that excels in all three areas is likely a strong choice.

6. *Prioritising prevention*: Invest time in understanding health insurance now to prevent future regrets. Making informed decisions about your coverage can spare you from financial distress when you need insurance the most.

By following these steps and prioritising understanding and informed decision-making, you're not just purchasing an insurance policy—you're securing your financial well-being and peace of mind for the future.

Exclusions

Understanding health insurance exclusions is crucial for every financially smart individual. Here's a guide to what your policy may not cover:

1. *Cosmetic surgeries*: Procedures like Botox, liposuction and implants, primarily for cosmetic reasons, are typically excluded. However, exceptions may apply if these surgeries are medically necessary.

2. *Pre-existing illnesses*: Many policies have waiting periods for pre-existing diseases (PED) before coverage begins, ranging from 12 to 48 months. Some newer plans offer PED coverage from Day 1.

3. *Infertility and pregnancy complications*: Basic health plans may not cover hospitalisation expenses related to infertility treatments, pregnancy complications or abortions. Specialised maternity or women's health plans might offer coverage for these expenses.

4. *Health supplements*: Health tonics and supplements without a doctor's prescription are usually not covered unless recommended by a treating physician.

5. *Alcohol-related illnesses*: Illnesses linked to excessive alcohol consumption, like liver damage, might not be covered.

6. *Alternative therapies*: Expenses for alternative therapies like naturopathy, acupuncture and reflexology are often excluded.

7. *Diagnostic charges*: Charges for diagnostic tests, scans and blood tests might not be covered unless specified by the policy or deemed necessary for treatment.

8. *Other exclusions*: Certain treatments like dental work might not be covered. Being aware of what's excluded can prevent unpleasant shocks.

Price vs Benefits

Choosing the right health insurance policy can feel like deciphering a secret code. But fear not, we're here to unravel the mystery in a way that's clear and relatable.

Think of health insurance as a smart investment. You pay a premium, and in return, you get protection from potentially hefty medical bills. Remember Rajesh? He got a health cover of ₹3 lakhs, thinking it'd be enough since he lived in a smaller town with lower costs. However, when he needed surgery, he realised a higher cover was necessary to safeguard his finances.

Now, let's meet Aunt Meera. She had knee pain before getting her policy. Her policy had a waiting period for pre-existing diseases. This meant she couldn't claim knee-related expenses in the initial years. If you have a pre-existing condition, it's crucial to check the waiting period—a little research now can save you surprises later.

Then there's Sunita. Her policy had sub-limits, meaning certain expenses, like room rent, had a cap. She ended up paying more because she chose a higher-category room without knowing about this.

Now, imagine Ritu, who didn't claim for a year. Her policy rewarded her with a no-claims bonus, increasing her coverage by 10% without a premium hike. It's like a little celebration for taking good care of yourself.

Some companies that encourage wellness offer plans that reward you for staying active. More steps mean a lower premium. It's like they're saying, 'We value your health, so we'll lighten your premium.'

Co-pay means sharing the bill with the insurer. If you have a 10% co-pay and a 1 lakh bill, you'll pay 10,000, and the insurer will cover the rest. Daycare procedures are treatments you don't need to stay overnight for. If you have a surgery and can go home the same day, that's a daycare procedure.

Lastly, don't fall into the tax-saving trap. While tax benefits are enticing, remember that health insurance offers more than just deductions. Uncle Harish and Aunt Sonal thought their retirement plan had them covered—until their company policy changed due to a takeover, and they were left without insurance when Uncle Harish fell ill. It's about securing peace of mind, not just saving tax.

Deciphering health insurance is like solving a puzzle. Price, benefits, waiting periods and sub-limits—every piece matters. Just as you would take time to find the perfect outfit, invest time in finding the right policy.

Seek expert advice, delve into the details and ask questions. Armed with knowledge, you're equipped to make a decision that ensures both your health and financial well-being.

Navigating Health Insurance with Pre-Existing Conditions: A Strategic Guide

Meet Priya, a vibrant thirty-eight-year-old woman determined to protect both her health and financial stability. Despite her proactive approach, Priya faced an unexpected challenge—she was denied health coverage due to a pre-existing thyroid condition. Frustrated but unwavering, she sought advice from a financial mentor and embarked on a unique strategy.

If you find yourself in a situation like Priya's, where a pre-existing condition complicates your pursuit of health insurance, there's still a path forward. As a financially astute woman, you can adopt strategies to ensure that you and your loved ones are adequately safeguarded. Consider these options:

1. *Consider policies with sub-limits*: Investigate health insurance policies that provide coverage, albeit with sub-limits for specific diseases or treatments. While these sub-

limits impose certain limitations, they offer a safety net for unexpected medical costs.

2. *Assess co-pay clauses*: Explore policies that feature co-pay clauses, requiring you to share a portion of the claim amount with the insurance company. This approach extends partial coverage while enabling you to manage financial obligations.

3. *Evaluate exclusion periods*: Familiarise yourself with exclusion periods, which involve waiting periods during which the policy won't cover claims related to pre-existing conditions. This awareness empowers you to plan effectively.

4. *Create a health corpus*: Establish a health corpus—a separate fund dedicated to health-related emergencies. Systematically invest in a balanced mutual fund over time, allowing your investments to grow and provide a financial cushion.

5. *Seek professional guidance*: Engage a financial advisor or mentor who possesses expertise in insurance and investments. Their guidance can help you devise a tailored strategy that aligns with your financial aspirations and health considerations.

Just as Priya's forward-thinking approach shielded her when health challenges emerged, your proactive steps can provide security and tranquillity. By exploring customised health insurance options, seeking expert guidance and establishing a health corpus, you embody the essence of financial intelligence. As a financially smart woman, you're prepared to tackle uncertainties head-on and make strategic decisions that safeguard your well-being and secure your financial future.

Smart Insurance Strategies for Older Women and Dependents

As we age, ensuring comprehensive health coverage becomes increasingly crucial, especially for older women and dependents aged sixty-six and above. Adequate health insurance can bring peace of mind amidst the rising costs of medical care. However, obtaining suitable coverage can be challenging due to age-related limitations and pre-existing conditions. Here are some strategic approaches for older women, single individuals and those with dependents to navigate health insurance obstacles effectively:

1. *Exploring top-up plans: Boosting coverage affordably.* Top-up plans offer a smart solution for enhancing health coverage without straining your budget. Suppose you have an existing policy covering 4 lakhs, and you purchase a top-up plan of 10 lakhs with a 4-lakh deductible. In that case, you're protected up to 4 lakhs by your base policy. For expenses beyond that, the top-up plan kicks in, ensuring comprehensive coverage. Even for scenarios involving multiple admissions, like three instances of 1 lakh each, a top-up plan safeguards your financial well-being.

2. *Harnessing group insurance: A collective shield.* Single women and those with older dependents can explore group insurance options through family members or their children's employers. Many companies extend health insurance coverage to employees' parents and parents-in-law. By aligning with this opportunity, you can bridge coverage gaps and ensure your well-being. Collaborating with your children to include you in their group insurance policy can provide substantial benefits, allowing you to access comprehensive coverage at a more affordable rate.

3. *Creating a personal medical fund: A safety net of your own.* For individuals facing challenges in acquiring suitable health insurance, creating a dedicated medical fund is a viable alternative. Setting aside funds in a disciplined manner enables you to accumulate resources to address medical expenses when needed. While this approach requires consistent commitment, it empowers you with financial preparedness, granting you the flexibility to manage health-related costs without undue stress.

4. *Engaging expert consultation: Tailored solutions.* Navigating health insurance options, especially as an older woman or a guardian of dependents, can be intricate. Seeking guidance from financial advisors or insurance experts can make a significant difference. They can help you explore tailored solutions, evaluate available options and make informed decisions that align with your specific circumstances and requirements.

In conclusion, securing adequate health coverage for older women and dependents is a crucial step towards financial resilience. Whether through top-up plans, group insurance, personal medical funds or expert guidance, these strategies empower you to proactively address health insurance challenges. By understanding your options, you lay the foundation for a secure and confident future, ensuring that you and your loved ones are safeguarded against unforeseen medical expenses.

Enhancing Your Health Insurance: Exploring Vital Riders for Comprehensive Coverage

In the realm of health insurance, riders stand as powerful tools to bolster your coverage, providing additional benefits that can prove invaluable in times of need. Riders, essentially add-ons to your health insurance policy, offer enhanced protection and customisation tailored to your unique needs. Let's delve into some of the most significant riders that can enhance your health insurance plan:

1. *Maternity cover rider: Nurturing well-being from conception to parenthood.* The maternity cover rider offers solace to those embarking on the journey of parenthood. Encompassing childbirth, pre- and post-natal expenses and even coverage for newborn baby expenses, this rider addresses the financial aspect of welcoming a new life. While it's important to note that this rider usually entails a waiting period ranging from two to six years, it is a pivotal addition for couples planning to expand their families.

2. *Critical illness rider: Shielding against life-altering ailments.* The critical illness rider guards against the financial upheaval caused by major illnesses such as heart attacks, cancer and more. Upon diagnosis of a covered critical illness during the policy tenure, this rider bestows a lump sum benefit, irrespective of the actual medical costs. With a waiting period of ninety days and a survival period of thirty days, this rider offers coverage for ten to forty critical diseases, depending on the insurer.

3. *Personal accident rider: Safeguarding against unexpected mishaps.* Life's uncertainties can manifest in unexpected accidents. The personal accident rider offers a safety net by providing compensation in case of accidental injuries leading to disability or even death. This rider covers permanent total disability with the entire sum insured and partial disability with a portion of the sum insured. Often referred to as the double indemnity rider, it extends

additional death benefits to your family in the case of accidental demise.

4. *Hospital cash rider: Financial support for incidental expenses.* When hospitalisation becomes a necessity, incidental expenses can add up quickly. The hospital cash rider comes to the rescue by providing a fixed daily cash allowance to cover these unforeseen costs during your hospital stay. In cases of ICU admission, this rider offers double the coverage amount for a specific duration. Remember, activation of this rider usually requires a hospital stay of at least twenty-four hours.

5. *Room rent waiver: Unrestricted choice for hospital accommodation.* This rider eliminates room rent caps, enabling you to opt for higher sub-limits or even no sub-limits for your hospital room without incurring additional expenses. You can then focus on receiving the best care without financial constraints dictating your choices.

Exploring these riders and understanding their intricacies empowers you to safeguard your well-being and financial stability effectively. Prioritise your health, anticipate uncertainties and embrace riders as allies in your pursuit of a secure and resilient future.

As we consider the significance of riders, the question arises: Should you opt for critical illness and accident cover in addition to your health insurance?

Absolutely, opting for critical illness and personal accident cover in addition to your health insurance can provide crucial financial protection in times of need. Critical illnesses like cancer can indeed lead to significant financial burdens due to the high costs of treatment and potential loss of income during recovery. Having a critical illness rider ensures that you receive a lump sum benefit upon diagnosis, helping to cover medical expenses and other financial obligations.

Similarly, accidents can occur unexpectedly and may result in temporary or permanent disability, impacting your ability to work and earn. A personal accident rider offers compensation in such scenarios, providing financial support to cover medical expenses, rehabilitation costs and other necessary expenses.

While standalone personal accident policies are advisable, adding a rider to your existing health insurance policy can offer an extra layer of protection without the need for separate premium payments. By exploring these riders and understanding their intricacies, you can enhance your overall coverage and strengthen your risk management strategy.

Prioritising your health and anticipating uncertainties are essential steps in securing comprehensive coverage and ensuring financial stability. Embracing riders as allies in your journey towards a secure future can provide peace of mind knowing that you and your loved ones are adequately protected against unforeseen circumstances.

Portability of Individual Health Insurance Policies

Health insurance portability allows policyholders to transfer their existing health insurance policies from one insurer to another without losing the benefits of the previous policy, such as waiting periods for pre-existing conditions. This ensures continuity of coverage and can provide better terms or services from the new insurer.

Here's a summary of the key points to keep in mind when considering portability:

1. *Continuation of benefits*: Existing policy benefits, including coverage for pre-existing conditions and waiting periods, are retained when switching insurers.
2. *No loss of cumulative bonus*: Accumulated no-claim bonuses (NCB) are carried forward to the new policy, potentially leading to reduced premiums or enhanced coverage.
3. *Easy switching process*: Insurance regulatory authorities have streamlined the porting process, with clear guidelines provided by the new insurer for a smoother transition.
4. *Porting request timeline*: Initiate the porting process at least forty-five days before the renewal date of the existing policy to allow sufficient time for document transfer and processing.

Medical insurance portability gives individuals better coverage and services, as it enables them to explore insurance plans from different providers to find one that best suits their needs. Switching to a policy with competitive premiums without losing previous benefits can lead to cost savings too, while coverage for pre-existing conditions is carried forward, potentially avoiding waiting periods in a new policy. Retaining the no-claim bonus from the previous policy can result in reduced premiums in the new policy, further contributing to cost savings.

Dos for Clients When Considering Portability

1. *Research extensively*: Compare offerings from various insurers to find the most suitable policy.
2. *Understand policy terms*: Familiarise yourself with policy terms, including coverage limits, exclusions and waiting periods.

3. *Apply in advance*: Initiate the porting process early to prevent coverage gaps.
4. *Provide accurate information*: Ensure all information provided during the porting process is accurate and complete to avoid complications later.

Don'ts for Clients When Considering Portability

1. *Don't let the policy lapse*: Ensure continuity of coverage by not letting the existing policy lapse before the new one takes effect.
2. *Don't hide health information*: Be truthful about medical history and pre-existing conditions to avoid claim rejection.
3. *Don't rush the decision*: Take time to understand the new policy before deciding.
4. *Don't forget to check network hospitals*: Ensure the new policy's network hospitals align with preferred healthcare providers for convenient access to services.

Remember to consult with insurance professionals or regulatory authorities for specific guidelines and regulations in your jurisdiction to make informed decisions regarding medical insurance portability.

For comprehensive guidelines on migration, refer to IRDA circular on portability or check with your HR or a qualified financial coach.[6])

---

6 'Circular: Norms on Renewability, Portability and Migration of Standard COVID Specific', *Insurance Regulatory and Development Authority of India*, 13 October 2020, https://irdai.gov.in/web/guest/document-detail?documentId=395568.

Mastering Health Insurance

As you emerge from this chapter, armed with knowledge and insights, you're not merely selecting a health insurance policy—you're paving the way towards financial peace of mind. With the appropriate health coverage, you're empowered to confront life's challenges head on, knowing that your financial stability remains steadfast.

Consider the meticulousness of a pilot before take-off or a surgeon in the operating room—they rely on checklists to ensure every crucial aspect is addressed, minimising risks and enhancing efficiency. Checklists are indispensable tools that help professionals stay organised, make informed decisions and mitigate potential pitfalls, whether soaring thousands of feet above the ground or performing intricate surgeries.

Applying this concept to your personal finance journey, particularly in the realm of health insurance, can yield significant benefits. A checklist empowers you to approach health coverage systematically, considering every factor contributing to your financial security. By following a structured approach, you can confidently navigate the complexities of health insurance, ensuring that you and your loved ones are adequately protected against unexpected medical expenses.

Health Insurance Checklist for Women

✓ *Assess your needs*: Understand your family's health needs, considering factors like age, medical history and any pre-existing conditions. This will help you determine the coverage amount required.

✓ *Set your budget*: Decide how much you can comfortably allocate to health insurance premiums without straining your finances. Remember, while it's an investment, it should be sustainable.

✓ *Research and compare*: Use online platforms to compare policies from different insurers. Look beyond the premium—consider benefits, exclusions and waiting periods.

✓ *Check network hospitals*: Ensure the insurer's network hospitals include those in your preferred area. A good hospital network means convenient access to quality healthcare.

✓ *Scrutinise benefits*: Evaluate the benefits offered, such as coverage for pre- and post-hospitalisation expenses, daycare procedures and critical illnesses.

✓ *Analyse waiting periods*: Check waiting periods for pre-existing diseases and specific treatments. Opt for a policy with shorter waiting periods if possible.

✓ *Understand co-payments*: Learn about co-payment clauses. While these reduce premiums, be aware of the additional costs you might need to share during a claim.

✓ *Examine sub-limits*: Consider policies without sub-limits on room rent, doctor fees or specific treatments. Comprehensive coverage ensures you're not caught off guard.

✓ *No-claims bonus (NCB)*: Explore policies that offer NCB, which reward you with increased coverage for claim-free years. It's a great way to enhance your protection over time.

✓ *Review exclusions*: Thoroughly read the list of exclusions to understand what's not covered. This will prevent disappointments during claim settlements.

✓ *Seek expert advice*: If navigating through policies feels overwhelming, consult a financial coach or mentor. Their expertise can help you make an informed decision.

✓ *Disclose accurately*: Honesty is vital. Disclose all medical information, even if it raises your premium. This ensures your claims won't be denied later due to non-disclosure.

✓ *Read the fine print*: Take time to read the policy documents carefully. Don't hesitate to clarify doubts with the insurer before finalising the purchase.

✓ *Assess family needs*: If you're married and have children, consider a family floater plan that covers everyone under a single policy for added convenience.

✓ *Prioritise peace of mind*: While cost matters, remember that health insurance is an investment in peace of mind. Opt for the policy that aligns with your health needs and financial goals.

Safeguarding Your Legacy: Life Insurance

'The best inheritance a parent can give his children is a few minutes of his time each day.'

—O.A. Battista

LIFE IS UNPREDICTABLE, AND IT'S WISE TO PREPARE FOR THE unexpected. Enter life insurance—a vital tool providing crucial financial support and peace of mind for your loved ones during tough times. By understanding the ins and outs of life insurance, you ensure that your legacy lives on long after you're gone. In this chapter, we'll explore various aspects of life insurance, empowering you to make informed decisions.

Understanding the Purpose of Life Insurance

Real-life incidents we witness around us or hear about in the news remind us of life's unpredictability. A young, health-conscious mother is suddenly diagnosed with a life-threatening illness. Her health deteriorates rapidly within a month and she passes away, leaving her family reeling. A diligent colleague, who always follows traffic rules, is involved in a car accident due to a reckless driver. These examples highlight the unpredictable nature of life and the importance of being prepared.

Accidents, illnesses and untimely deaths don't discriminate—they affect the unsuspecting and cautious alike. Recognising this reality is crucial for making informed financial decisions, especially regarding life insurance. However, navigating life insurance can be daunting due to misguidance or unqualified advice.

You might end up with excessive premiums and inadequate coverage. You might mistakenly believe that you're invulnerable to life's uncertainties, influenced by changing advisors or inconsistent advice. The fundamental issue is underestimating life's unpredictable nature.

Life insurance is more than just a financial product; it's for a sign of care for your family's well-being. While it can't replace the physical and emotional loss of a death in the family, it provides a safety net against financial hardships, ensuring your loved ones are supported even in your absence.

Remember the story of Sheena which we read at the start of the book, a successful professional and friend who unexpectedly lost her husband Tarun during the COVID-19 pandemic? Tarun's passing left Sheena to deal with the aftermath of his financial decisions, including inadequate life insurance coverage and mounting debts. Despite her efforts, Sheena faced financial hardships.

Reflecting on Sheena's story, it's evident that financial literacy and preparedness are paramount. None of us knows what the future holds, but we can take steps to be ready for whatever comes our way. By investing time in ourselves and making informed choices, we can ensure a better future for ourselves and our families.

Life insurance isn't about fear—it's about securing your family's financial future. Rise above confusion and make term life insurance the foundation of your risk management plan.

Visualising Your Legacy: Evaluating Your Life Insurance Needs

Now, let's engage in a thought-provoking exercise—envisioning a life without your spouse or you. Imagine the situation your loved ones will be in if either of you aren't there. This will show clearly how important life insurance is in securing their future. By visualising your legacy, you gain clarity on your life insurance needs and reaffirm your commitment to safeguarding your family's future.

Close your eyes and step into an alternate reality. Imagine a life where you no longer exist—a life without your presence, guidance and income. Visualise your spouse, child and dependants navigating a world now devoid of your support. Picture them grappling with questions that were once distant concerns. Witness the emotional upheaval as your spouse grapples with grief and loss. Envision the strain of adjusting to a life without your companionship.

Observe the financial challenges your loved ones face. Your income that once paid EMIs, covered bills and funded dreams is no more. The burden of loans, the weight of creditors and the uncertain future now hangs over them. How does the loss of your financial support alter your family's lifestyle? Picture the compromises they may need to make, the dreams they must shelve and the sacrifices they endure.

Imagine the impact on your children's education and aspirations. Envision them potentially needing to abandon dreams due to financial constraints. Reflect on the quality of life your loved ones might experience in your absence. Consider their challenges in maintaining their current standard of living.

This exercise, though difficult, underscores the critical importance of life insurance in ensuring your family's stability and security in your absence. It emphasizes the need for proactive financial planning to protect the future of those you cherish.

Turning Vision into Action: Planning Your Legacy

As the exercise concludes, step out of that alternate reality, and bring the lessons learnt back into the present. The life drill isn't meant to evoke fear or distress; it's a tool for empowerment. It's a wake-up call that urges you to overcome complacency and take charge of your family's well-being.

1. *Defining your legacy*: Imagine revisiting that alternate reality, this time as an active participant. What changes do you wish to implement to ensure a smoother path for your loved ones? What improvements do you envision for their financial and emotional well-being?

2. *Creating your blueprint*: This introspective journey serves as a blueprint for your life insurance needs. It shapes your decisions, prompts discussions with your family and guides your action plan.

3. *Choosing the right life cover*: Armed with a deeper understanding of the impact of your absence, you can now select an appropriate life insurance cover. A term life insurance policy becomes a shield that safeguards your

family's financial stability and allows them to uphold their aspirations, even in your absence.

4. *Empowerment through planning*: This exercise transforms your perspective on life insurance from a mere financial obligation to a profound commitment to your loved ones' well-being.

We have now embarked on a journey of introspection—a journey that encourages you to step into a world where you are not present, and in doing so, uncover the significance of life insurance. The life drill isn't meant to dwell on the inevitable, but rather to equip you with the clarity and motivation needed to shape your legacy. Through the prism of this exercise, you can now evaluate your life insurance needs with a newfound understanding and purpose. Your life insurance cover becomes more than a policy; it transforms into a testament to your unwavering commitment to securing your loved one's future, even in your absence.

Decoding Life Insurance Products: Empowering Your Financial Choices

An array of life insurance products is available in the market. This section aims to unravel the mystery surrounding these products, debunk myths and empower you to make informed decisions that align with your financial goals. Let's delve into the intricacies of different life insurance plans, starting with the widely misunderstood yet indispensable term insurance.

Traditional vs Pure Life Insurance Policies: Making an Informed Choice

Before selecting a life insurance product, you need to understand the distinction between traditional and pure life insurance policies.

Traditional policies, where investment is mixed with insurance

- Combine insurance coverage with an investment component;
- Offer features like bonuses and loyalty additions that enhance returns;
- Are suited for individuals seeking both insurance protection and a savings component.

On the other hand, pure life insurance policies, or term plans

- Provide straightforward insurance coverage without any investment component;
- Offer higher coverage at lower premiums compared to traditional policies;
- Are ideal for individuals solely focused on securing their family's financial future in case of the policyholder's demise.

What this means is that in a term plan, you pay a predetermined premium, and in return, your family receives a predetermined sum assured if you pass away during the policy's term.

Choosing the Right Policy

Selecting between traditional and pure life insurance policies depends on your financial objectives and priorities. If you aim to blend insurance protection with a savings element, traditional policies or ULIPs may suit you, provided you're aware of their charges and relatively lower risk coverage. Conversely, if you are looking for maximum coverage at a lower cost, term plans offer a straightforward solution.

Making an informed decision demands a clear grasp of your financial aspirations and needs. Seeking advice from a financial advisor can offer valuable insights and aid in selecting the policy type that matches your goals.

If maintaining discipline with long-term investments is challenging or you're susceptible to market fluctuations, and if you're unwilling to take calculated risks or leverage compounding benefits, an investment-oriented traditional insurance plan may be preferable. While such plans may yield lower returns, they serve as a vehicle for savings, preventing premature fund withdrawals due to policy conditions. It's crucial to invest in them knowingly, aligning with your risk appetite and goals.

For financially astute women, self-awareness and understanding the why behind financial decisions are crucial. It's advisable to refrain from mixing investments with insurance. Instead, consider utilising insurance returns as part of your debt portfolio. Pure term life insurance often stands out as the most effective form of life insurance, offering comprehensive coverage without the complexities of investment components.

Why Term Insurance Plans Are Essential

Term insurance policies may sometimes seem like a waste of money, but this is not so; they serve as an investment in your family's future. While term plans don't offer financial returns like investment-linked policies, their purpose is clear—to safeguard your family's financial stability in your absence.

Consider the scenario of Maya, a married working woman with dependent children. Recognising the importance of her income for her family's financial security, she opts for a term insurance policy with a sum assured of ₹1 crore. This policy serves as a safety net for her family, covering their day-to-day expenses, children's education and any other financial needs that may arise in the event of her demise. Essentially, term insurance provides peace of mind and financial stability for Maya and her loved ones.

Different Life Insurance Products

While term insurance lays the foundation for financial protection, various life insurance products offer a blend of insurance coverage and investment opportunities. Let's delve deeper into these alternatives, highlighting their features, benefits and considerations.

1. Term Life Insurance

Term life insurance provides pure life cover for a specified period. If the person insured passes away during the policy term, the sum assured is paid to the beneficiaries.

Benefits

- ✓ *High coverage at low cost*: This policy offers high coverage at affordable premiums.
- ✓ *Simplicity*: Straightforward and cost-effective, it provides essential financial protection for your family.

This is ideal for individuals looking for maximum coverage for a specific period, such as covering loan liabilities, children's education, or expenses until retirement.

2. Endowment Plans

Endowment plans combine insurance with savings. A portion of the premium goes towards coverage, and the remaining is invested, resulting in a lump sum payout on maturity.

Benefits

- ✓ *Maturity benefit*: Provides a lump-sum payout at maturity if the policyholder survives the term.
- ✓ *Forced savings*: Encourages disciplined savings, suitable for those who struggle to save regularly.

Considerations

- ✓ *Lower returns*: Returns tend to be lower compared to pure investment avenues.
- ✓ *Higher premiums*: Premiums are relatively higher due to the combination of insurance and savings components.

This is suitable for those looking for a combination of protection and savings, but with lower coverage compared to term plans.

3. Whole Life Insurance

Whole life insurance provides coverage for the entire lifetime of the insured. It offers a death benefit to the beneficiaries and sometimes accumulates a cash value over time.

Benefits

- ✓ *Lifelong coverage*: Provides coverage for the insured's entire life.
- ✓ *Savings component*: May accumulate cash value, which can be borrowed against or withdrawn.

This is more suitable for estate planning, wealth transfer and long-term financial goals.

4. Money-Back Policies

Money-back policies provide periodic payouts to the policyholder during the policy term. These payouts offer liquidity and cater to short-term financial needs.

Benefits

- ✓ *Liquidity*: Provides periodic cash flows for various life milestones.
- ✓ *Insurance cover*: In case of the policyholder's demise, the nominee receives the sum assured.

Considerations

- ✓ *Reduced returns*: Overall returns may be lower compared to pure investment options due to periodic payouts.
- ✓ *Higher premiums*: Premiums tend to be higher than term insurance due to the payouts.

This is suitable for those seeking a regular income during the policy term and coverage for their family's financial needs.

5. Unit-Linked Insurance Plans (ULIPs)

ULIPs are a dynamic blend of insurance and investment, allowing policyholders to allocate funds to various investment options such as equity, debt or balanced funds.

Benefits

- ✓ *Investment flexibility*: Offers choices catering to different risk profiles and financial goals.

✓ *Market-linked returns*: Returns are linked to the performance of the chosen investment funds.

Considerations

✓ *Charges*: Involves charges like premium allocation, fund management and policy administration, which can impact returns.
✓ *Risk exposure*: The investment component exposes policyholders to market volatility, affecting the value of the investment.

This is suitable for those looking for a combination of insurance and market-linked investment opportunities, with a higher risk tolerance.

Understanding different types of life insurance policies is crucial for making informed decisions about your financial protection. Choose a policy that aligns with your financial goals, risk appetite and coverage needs to ensure comprehensive financial security for you and your loved ones.

Choosing the Right Option: A Balancing Act

When considering life insurance products beyond term plans, it's vital to assess your financial goals, risk tolerance and liquidity requirements. While endowment assurance policies offer a combination of savings and insurance, money-back policies provide periodic liquidity. ULIPs offer investment opportunities but also involve market risks.

Here are some key factors to consider:

1. *Financial goals*: Determine whether you're seeking insurance coverage, savings or investment growth. Understanding

your financial objectives will help you choose a policy that best meets your needs and aspirations.

2.   *Risk tolerance*: Evaluate your comfort level with market volatility and investment risk. Different life insurance products carry varying levels of risk, so it's essential to choose one that aligns with your risk tolerance and investment preferences.

3.   *Liquidity needs*: Consider your need for periodic payouts or access to funds. Depending on your financial situation and future plans, you may require liquidity at different stages of your life. Assessing your liquidity needs will help you select a policy that offers the flexibility you require.

4.   *Informed decision-making*: Take a holistic approach to decision-making by considering all aspects of each life insurance product. Understand the features, benefits and drawbacks of different policies to make an informed choice that suits your unique circumstances.

As you explore life insurance options beyond term plans, remember that each product has its unique features and benefits. It's essential to align your choice with your financial aspirations and priorities. Consulting with a qualified financial advisor can provide valuable insights and guidance, helping you make an informed decision that harmonises insurance coverage, savings and investment potential to secure your family's financial future.

Bonus and Loyalty Addition in Traditional Life Insurance Policies

When exploring traditional life insurance policies, terms like 'bonus' and 'loyalty addition' frequently emerge. These components are instrumental in augmenting the returns of such policies, making them more attractive. Let's delve into the significance of these terms and how they bolster the benefits of your policy:

Bonus: A share of profits

Bonuses represent a portion of the profits earned by the insurance company, distributed among policyholders who possess participating policies. These policies are eligible to partake in the company's profits, which primarily stem from the insurer's investment endeavours and favourable claims experience.

Some common types of bonuses include:

- *Simple reversionary bonus*: Declared annually, this bonus is added to the policy's sum assured. Once declared, it becomes guaranteed and is payable upon maturity or death.
- *Compound reversionary bonus*: Calculated as a percentage of the accumulated sum assured and previously declared bonuses, this bonus compounds each year.

Bonuses offer dual benefits. First, they contribute to the enhanced maturity value of the policy, thereby augmenting overall returns. Second, they provide a risk-free addition to the policy, ensuring additional payouts irrespective of market fluctuations.

Loyalty addition: Rewarding long-term commitment

Loyalty addition is an extra amount paid to policyholders who have maintained their policies for a specific duration, typically exceeding a decade. It serves as a token of appreciation from the insurance company for the policyholder's steadfast loyalty and commitment over the years.

A loyalty addition includes a reward for long-term holding, which is an additional payout for long-term policyholders. It also includes encouragement for persistence, which serve to incentivise policyholders to continue their policy, reassuring them that their dedication will be duly acknowledged with an extra reward.

Bonuses and loyalty additions are pivotal elements of traditional life insurance policies, fostering a symbiotic relationship between policyholders and insurance companies while enriching the overall value of the policy.

The Pitfalls of Mixing Investment and Insurance: 'IIMB' and 'KILB'

In the realm of life insurance, avoiding certain pitfalls is crucial for maintaining adequate coverage and financial security. Two such pitfalls are IIMB, or *investment insurance mix karne ki bimaari* (the illness of mixing insurance and investment), and KILB, or *kam insurance lene ki bimaari* (the illness of taking less insurance), representing misguided approaches to insurance planning.

Let's explore these pitfalls and their implications through a real-life example, as introduced by Religare Insurance Company in their advertisement campaigns.

IIMB often leads individuals to allocate a significant portion of their premium towards investment-linked policies rather than focusing on the primary purpose of insurance—protecting the financial future of their dependents.

One consequence of IIMB is insufficient coverage—by prioritising investment, policyholders may end up with inadequate life coverage, leaving their family vulnerable in the event of an unforeseen demise.

Another consequence is a misalignment of goals. When investment objectives overshadow the primary goal of insurance, the intended safety net for loved ones gets compromised.

KILB signifies the inclination to opt for minimal insurance coverage due to concerns about premium payments. This often results in individuals selecting policies with lower coverage than what their family truly needs.

KILB can have two consequences. The first is inadequate protection, as the policy may not provide sufficient funds to meet various financial obligations in the absence of the policyholder. The second is a false sense of security: having a policy may lead to an attitude that doesn't prioritise savings, while the insurance coverage will prove inadequate when the need arises, leaving the loved ones stranded without funds.

Maya's case vividly illustrates the repercussions of inadequate insurance coverage, particularly due to the KILB mindset. Her husband's decision to choose lower premiums over sufficient coverage left the family in a precarious situation after his untimely demise. Despite having some financial assistance from the policy, it was woefully inadequate to meet the family's needs.

The consequences were severe—Maya and her children faced financial hardship, struggled to cover daily expenses, fulfil education costs and manage loan obligations. Because of this, Maya was forced to return to work prematurely and experienced both emotional and financial strain.

This unfortunate scenario underscores the importance of obtaining adequate insurance coverage. Opting for minimal coverage to save on premiums may seem appealing in the short term, but it can have devastating long-term consequences. Adequate coverage ensures that loved ones are protected and provided for in times of crisis, preventing undue financial burden and emotional distress.

The Rule of 72: A Practical Tool for Financial Decision-Making

The Rule of 72 is a quick and handy way to assess whether investment promises are realistic or not. This versatile rule helps you cut through the confusion of large numbers and make sense of investment claims. Here's how it works.

To determine the annual rate of return required for any 'double-your-money' proposition, ask, 'How long will it take for my money to double?' Then, simply divide 72 by that number of years. For example, if an agent claims your ₹1 lakh will grow to ₹2 lakhs in fifteen years, dividing 72 by 15 gives you an approximate annual return of 4.8%. This calculation provides a quick check that aligns closely with more precise calculations, which is 4.73%.

This formula is a valuable tip to stay aware and alert in financial decision-making. It can also be applied to understand inflation rates—how many years it takes for inflation to double your costs—and to recognise potentially risky schemes promising unrealistic returns, like Ponzi schemes.

Avoiding the Investment-Insurance Mix-Up

Insurance and investment serve distinct purposes in financial planning. Insurance protects your family's future, providing financial security in case of unforeseen events, while investments aim to grow your wealth over time. Understanding the differences and avoiding the pitfalls of mixing these two can significantly impact your long-term financial health.

Traditional life insurance policies often include an investment component that can blur the lines between insurance and wealth creation. While these policies offer savings and returns, they may not always be the most efficient way to achieve both financial security and growth. Term insurance, with its straightforward coverage without investment features, remains a solid foundation for your family's financial protection.

Term insurance emerges as the cornerstone of your family's financial security, thanks to its simplicity. Other products like endowment assurance policies, money-back policies and ULIPs each come with unique features and considerations.

With a grasp of concepts like the Rule of 72, bonus and loyalty additions and the differences between traditional and pure life insurance policies, you gain a comprehensive understanding of your options. Remember to avoid mixing investment and insurance, making decisions aligned with your long-term financial goals. Armed with this knowledge, you can navigate the landscape of life insurance products confidently, ensuring the well-being of your loved ones.

Determining Your Coverage Needs

The amount of life insurance coverage you need depends on various factors specific to your financial situation and family's needs. Consider the following factors when determining your coverage needs:

1. *Income replacement*: Calculate the amount of money your family would require to maintain their current living standards and cover essential expenses if you were to pass away. This includes ongoing expenses like mortgage or rent, utilities, groceries.

2. *Debts and liabilities*: Consider any outstanding debts you have, such as mortgages, car loans or personal loans. Your life insurance coverage should be sufficient to pay off these debts to ensure your family isn't burdened financially.

3. *Education and future goals*: Factor in the cost of education for your children, including school fees, college tuition and other educational expenses. Additionally, consider any major life events you anticipate, such as weddings or purchasing a home.

4. *Final expenses*: Account for funeral and burial costs, as well as any other end-of-life expenses. These expenses can add up quickly and should be included in your coverage amount.

5. *Healthcare and emergency funds*: Ensure that your coverage includes funds for medical expenses and emergency situations. Having adequate coverage ensures your family can pay off unexpected medical bills or emergencies.

6. *Inflation*: Keep in mind that the cost of living tends to increase over time due to inflation. Adjust your coverage amount to account for inflation and ensure that your policy's payout maintains its value over the years.

By carefully considering these factors and assessing your family's needs, you can determine the life insurance cover that's right for you. Review your coverage periodically and make adjustments as required.

The Right Time to Buy Life Insurance—The Sooner, the Better

When it comes to buying life insurance, the golden rule is the sooner, the better. Life insurance premiums are usually lower when you're young and healthy. As you age, the cost of coverage increases due to a higher risk of health issues. Moreover, purchasing life insurance early ensures your loved ones are protected right from the start.

For example, if a healthy woman named Shalini, aged thirty, decides to purchase a term life insurance policy with a coverage amount of ₹50 lakh for a twenty-year term, her premium for this policy might be around ₹15,000 per year.

If Shalini waits until she's forty to purchase the same policy, her premium might increase to around ₹25,000 per year.

If Shalini waits until she's fifty, her premium might increase further to around ₹40,000 per year.

This increase in the cost of the premium is typically due to factors such as increased mortality risk and the shorter remaining coverage period. Therefore, it's advisable to purchase life insurance at a younger age to lock in lower premiums and ensure affordability of coverage over the long term.

Life Insurance and Taxes—Dispelling the Tax-Saving Myth

While it's true that life insurance can provide certain tax benefits, using it solely for tax saving is not the most effective strategy. The primary purpose of life insurance is to provide financial protection for your loved ones, so that should be the main objective when buying a policy. Tax saving shouldn't be the sole driver of your decisions. However, certain policies like term plans offer tax deductions under Section 80C of the Income Tax Act. It's crucial to consult a tax advisor to understand the tax implications of your life insurance choices.

Understanding Different Types of Life Insurance Policies

Understanding different types of life insurance policies is crucial for making informed decisions about your financial protection. Here's a breakdown of some common policies:

Term Life Insurance

✓ *Definition*: Term life insurance provides pure life coverage for a specified period, known as the term. If the person insured passes away during the policy term, the sum assured is paid to the beneficiaries.
✓ *Benefits*: Term plans offer high coverage at affordable premiums. They are straightforward and cost-effective, providing essential financial protection for your family.
✓ *Scenario*: Ideal for individuals looking for maximum coverage for a specific period, such as covering loan liabilities, children's education or expenses until retirement.

Endowment Plans

✓ *Definition*: Endowment plans combine insurance with savings. A portion of the premium goes towards coverage, and the remaining is invested, resulting in a lump sum payout on maturity.
✓ *Benefits*: These plans provide maturity benefits along with life coverage. They can be suitable for short- to

medium-term financial goals and offer a disciplined way to save.

✓ *Scenario*: Suitable for those looking for a combination of protection and savings, but with lower coverage compared to term plans.

Whole Life Insurance

✓ *Definition*: Whole life insurance provides coverage for the entire lifetime of the insured. It offers a death benefit to the beneficiaries and sometimes accumulates a cash value over time.

✓ *Benefits*: These policies offer lifelong coverage and can be considered as part of estate planning. They may also have a savings component.

✓ *Scenario*: More suitable for estate planning, wealth transfer and long-term financial goals.

Enhancing Coverage with Riders

Similar to health insurance, there are some riders that you can add to your base policy to improve the cover provided by the policy.

Critical Illness Rider

✓ *Definition*: Critical illness riders provide a lump sum amount upon diagnosis of critical illnesses like cancer, heart attack or stroke.

✓ *Benefits*: These riders offer financial support during major health crises, helping cover medical expenses and maintaining your family's financial stability.

Accidental Death and Disability Rider

- ✓ *Definition*: This rider provides an additional payout if the insured's death or disability is due to an accident.
- ✓ *Benefits*: Offers extra financial protection in case of accidental death or disability, helping your family manage unexpected challenges.

Regularly reviewing your life insurance policy is crucial for ensuring that it aligns with your changing circumstances. As you experience major life events like marriage, the birth of a child or a job change, your coverage needs may adapt. Periodic reviews help you adjust your coverage and beneficiaries accordingly.

Once you have gone through all of these steps to evaluate your needs and determined the product best suited for you, the next step is to choose the insurance provider. Choosing the right insurance provider is as important as selecting the right policy. Consider factors such as claim settlement ratio, financial stability, customer service and the range of products offered. Research and read customer reviews to make an informed decision.

Understanding When You May Not Need a Life Cover

While life insurance is essential for most individuals, there are scenarios where it may not be a top priority:

If you've reached a stage where your debts are cleared, and you're financially independent, the need for life insurance may reduce. If you're single with no dependents, the need for a substantial life cover will decrease as well. Once you're financially secure in retirement and no longer have significant financial responsibilities, you might consider reducing or discontinuing life coverage.

It's crucial to remember that the primary purpose of life insurance is to provide financial protection against untimely death. Pure term insurance serves this purpose most effectively. It offers high coverage at a reasonable cost, ensuring that your family's financial security is prioritised. Mixing insurance with investment might dilute the essential coverage you need, so focus on keeping them separate for optimal results.

As we navigate the intricate world of life insurance, it's vital to understand the various policy types, enhance coverage with appropriate riders and periodically review your policy. Selecting the right insurance provider and recognising when life coverage may not be necessary is equally important. Ultimately, the goal is to safeguard your family's future with the most effective tool—a pure term insurance policy.

Unveiling the World of Investments—Market Insights and Basics

'The individual investor should act consistently as an investor and not as a speculator.'

—Ben Graham

HEY THERE, AMAZING WOMEN! I WANT TO SHARE A BIT OF MY JOURNEY with you—a journey that started with a monthly income of ₹4500 and has seen the Sensex rise from 1,000 to a whopping 78,000 in June 2024.

Back when I began my career at the age of nineteen, the world seemed like a maze of uncertainties. From navigating through the Harshad Mehta scam to weathering global crises and pandemics, we have witnessed a spectrum of challenges. Amidst it all, I vividly remember the BSE Sensex reaching its then all-time high of 4,630.54 points in September 1994—such a crazy time, right?

In those days, fixed deposits were the talk of the town, with bank FD rates soaring to a staggering 13% during the 1990s. We found comfort in FDs, insurance policies, and post office schemes. The world of Sensex and stock markets seemed distant, something meant for others, not us.

Imagine if, back in 1994, I had started investing just ₹1,500 per month. With an average annual return of 14%, I would have attained a corpus of 1.05 crores over nearly thirty years. However, like many others, fear, lack of knowledge and the belief that the stock market wasn't for us held us back.

The current sky-high Sensex figure of 78,000 prompts reflections on missed opportunities and how different things might have been if we had taken that leap into the world of investments earlier.

So, my wonderful women, let me tell you—financial literacy is key. Don't let fear or lack of knowledge hold you back. There's a whole financial world out there, and it's time we take charge of our money. Start small, educate yourself and don't be afraid to explore new avenues. Whether it's investing in stocks and mutual funds or understanding the changing financial landscape, let's break those barriers together.

In my journey, I've learnt that being financially smart is not about the size of your income; it's about making informed choices and planning for the long run. So, let's empower ourselves, let's be financially smart women and let's create a future where we're in control of our financial destinies. You've got this!

Embarking on your investment odyssey has two aspects:

1. *Navigating the investment landscape*: Explore the fundamentals of markets and indices like Sensex, BSE

and NSE and grasp their role in shaping your investment journey.

2. *Exploring investment vehicles*: Gain an understanding of investment instruments, such as stocks, mutual funds, SIPs and lump-sum investments, and identify the best fit for your financial goals.

Welcome to the exciting world of investments, where your money has the potential to grow and work for you. In this chapter, we will guide you through the fundamental concepts of investments, helping you navigate the investment landscape with confidence and insight.

The Investment Landscape—Markets and Indices

Markets are dynamic platforms where the buying and selling of various financial instruments occur. The stock market is a prominent example, where shares of publicly listed companies are traded. The performance of the overall market is often represented by indices like the Sensex, BSE and NSE.

The Bombay Stock Exchange (BSE) is one of the oldest and largest stock exchanges in India, facilitating the trading of a wide range of securities. The BSE Sensex is a benchmark index that reflects the performance of thirty major companies listed on the BSE. It gives you an overview of how the top companies are faring in the market.

The National Stock Exchange (NSE) is another significant stock exchange, known for its electronic trading platform and diverse product offerings.

These indices provide crucial insights into the overall health of the market and serve as benchmarks for investment performance.

Exploring Investment Vehicles

Investment vehicles are like vehicles that take you on a financial journey to your goals. Let's understand some key ones:

- *Stocks (or shares)*: Think of stocks as a piece of a company that you own. When the company does well, your stock value rises. It's like being part-owner and sharing in the company's success. Similarly, when the company does badly, its value drops, and so does the value of your share of it—the stock prices fall. You can buy and sell various stocks on the market.
- *Mutual funds*: Imagine a team of experts managing a pool of money from various investors. That's what mutual funds are. They invest in a variety of stocks or other assets, spreading the risk and increasing the chances of good returns for everyone who has contributed to the pool. The returns are proportional to the quantum of investment.
- *SIP (systematic investment plan)*: SIP works like a tool that allows you to save consistently and smartly. Instead of putting a large sum all at once into mutual funds, you invest a fixed amount regularly. It's like taking small, steady steps toward your financial goals.
- *Lump-sum investments*: This is like making a big purchase in one go and involves investing a significant amount at once. It can be a great move if you have a lump sum amount available.

The trick is to match the vehicle with your destination. If you're looking for steady growth, mutual funds or SIPs could be your companions. If you're comfortable with risks and want potentially higher returns, stocks might be your route of choice.

Understanding these investment vehicles gives you the power to decide which one aligns with your goals, risk tolerance and financial journey.

As you embark on your investment journey, remember that knowledge is your greatest asset. Educate yourself about different investment options, stay updated on market trends and regularly assess your portfolio's performance. With a clear understanding of investment basics, you'll be better equipped to make informed decisions that pave the way for your financial future.

Clearing the Confusion: SIPs, Markets and Mutual Funds

Let me share this conversation I had with one of my high net-worth women prospects, Shivani, who was referred to me by a client.

She said, 'I've been hearing a lot about SIPs on the radio. I think I want to invest in SIPs, but I'm afraid of the markets. They seem so risky!'

I replied, 'I completely understand your concerns. Let's break down SIPs, markets and mutual funds to help you make an informed decision.'

Myth #1: SIP is a specific investment product

Financial Advisor: 'First, let's address the misconception. SIP stands for systematic investment plan. It's not a specific product, but rather a method of investing. Imagine it as a way of putting your money to work in small, regular amounts instead of one big lump sum.'

Shivani: 'Oh, I thought it was something I could just buy. So, how does it work?'

Financial Advisor: 'When you invest through an SIP, you're essentially contributing a fixed amount of money at regular intervals, such as every month. This way, you're not trying to predict market movements or timing your investments. It's a disciplined approach that helps you benefit from the power of compounding.'

Myth #2: SIPs and investing in markets are the same

Financial Advisor: 'Now, about your concerns regarding the markets. Investing through an SIP doesn't mean directly putting money into the stock market. SIPs can be used to invest in mutual funds, which are managed by experts.'

Shivani: 'But aren't mutual funds linked to the markets?'

Financial Advisor: 'Yes, they are. However, investing in mutual funds doesn't mean you're directly buying stocks. Mutual funds pool money from various investors to invest in a diversified portfolio. This diversification spreads the risk, reducing the impact of a single stock's performance on your investment.'

Myth #3: Safe savings vs investing

Financial Advisor: 'You mentioned you're keeping your money in savings accounts. While that's safe, the returns are usually very low. Investing, on the other hand, offers the potential for higher returns over the long term.'

Shivani: 'But isn't investing risky?'

Financial Advisor: 'Investing involves risks, but it's about managing those risks. Avoiding the markets entirely might mean missing out on opportunities for your money to grow. Plus, the longer you invest, the more time your investments have to recover from market fluctuations.'

Shivani: 'I've also been buying shares based on tips from friends and colleagues.'

Financial Advisor: 'Individual stock trading can be risky, especially if it's based on tips. Investing in mutual funds provides professional management and diversification, which can help you achieve more balanced returns.'

Shivani: 'I also want to plan a dream vacation. Can I do that through my investments?'

Financial Advisor: 'Absolutely, and that's a great goal. By creating a balanced financial plan that includes investing, you can work towards achieving both your short-term and long-term goals.'

Investing doesn't have to be as intimidating as it seems. SIPs and mutual funds are tools that can help you grow your wealth in a disciplined and managed manner. While all investments carry some level of risk, proper planning, diversification and a long-term approach can help you navigate these waters successfully. Remember, it's not about avoiding risks altogether, but about making informed choices to manage those risks effectively.

A Mindset for Building Wealth

The journey to financial empowerment for women extends beyond budgeting and saving—it needs to delve into investing too. We need to demystify the intricacies of investing, steering you away from the allure of day trading towards the steady path of building a healthy financial future.

Investing is not a mysterious realm reserved for financial experts or thrill-seekers. It's a strategic approach to growing wealth over the long term. Unlike the frenzy of day trading, where decisions are made in the heat of the moment, investing is a deliberate and calculated endeavour. Day trading involves buying and selling financial assets, such as stocks, within the same trading day. Traders aim to capitalise on short-term price fluctuations to make quick profits. Unlike long-term investing, where investors hold assets for an extended period, day traders typically close all their positions by the end of the trading day. This approach requires constant monitoring of market movements and often involves high levels of risk due to the volatile nature of short-term price changes.

While some apps entice users with the promise of free shares and the thrill of immediate gains, beware of the trap they set. Day trading may offer short-term highs, but it often leads to long-term lows. Day traders, driven by market fluctuations, tend to incur fees and taxes, which ultimately erode their wealth. Investing, on the other hand, should be anything but exhilarating; it's a stable and measured approach to wealth accumulation.

Investing is about setting up your financial future by putting your money to work for you automatically. Instead of constantly monitoring market trends, successful investors establish automated processes. They let their investments grow passively. An empowered rich life is not lived in front of a computer screen; it's lived beyond the spreadsheets, where financial well-being is just one component.

Navigating Tax Planning: A Roadmap to Financial Efficiency

'In this world nothing can be said to be certain, except death and taxes.'

—Benjamin Franklin

INDIA'S TAXATION SYSTEM IS MULTIFACETED, COMPRISING SEVERAL types of taxes such as income tax, goods and services tax (GST), and others. Navigating this landscape requires an understanding of tax slabs, exemptions, and specific considerations for different groups of women.

Tax slabs are predefined ranges of income on which different tax rates are applied. In India, the income tax system follows a progressive structure, meaning that the tax rate increases with higher income levels. Understanding these tax slabs is crucial for individuals to calculate their tax liability accurately. Let's explore the latest tax slabs and exemptions for women in the financial year 2023–24 to gain insights into how taxes are calculated and how certain exemptions can help reduce the overall tax burden.

In 2023, the government introduced various incentives to encourage the adoption of the new regime, which was first introduced in 2020. These changes indicate that the government intends for taxpayers to transition to the new regime and eventually phase out the old one. Though the new regime is now the default tax regime, the old tax regime will continue to exist.

No changes were made in direct taxes in the Interim Budget 2024–25. Let's look at both regimes and see which regime to opt for in 2024.

The New Tax Regime

In the new tax regime, taxpayers are offered concessional tax rates. However, those who opt for the new regime cannot claim several exemptions and deductions, such as HRA, LTA, 80C, 80D and more that are available in the older regime. Because of this, the new tax regime did not have many takers. The government introduced five key changes in the Budget 2023 to encourage taxpayers to adopt the new regime. They are:

1. *Higher tax rebate limit*: Full tax rebate on an income up to ₹7 lakhs has been introduced, compared to ₹5 lakhs under the old tax regime. This means that taxpayers with an income of up to ₹7 lakhs will not have to pay any tax at all under the new tax regime.
2. *Streamlined tax slabs*: The tax exemption limit has been increased to ₹3 lakhs, and the new tax slabs are:

Total Income	Rate of Tax
up to ₹3,00,000	Nil
₹3,00,001–₹6,00,000	5%
₹6,00,001–₹9,00,000	10%
₹9,00,001–₹12,00,000	15%
₹12,00,001–₹15,00,000	20%
₹15,00,001 and above	30%

Note: This is for women below sixty years in AY 2023–24. An additional health and education cess of 4% is payable on the income tax amount under both old and new tax regimes.

3. *Standard deduction and family pension deduction*
   - *Salary income*: The standard deduction of ₹50,000, which was only available under the old regime, has now been extended to the new tax regime as well. This, along with the rebate, makes an income up to ₹7.5 lakhs tax-free under the new regime.
   - *Family pension*: Those receiving a family pension can claim a deduction of ₹15,000 or one-third of the pension, whichever is lower.
4. *Reduced surcharge for high-net-worth individuals*: The surcharge rate on income over ₹5 crores has been reduced from 37% to 25%. This move will bring down their effective tax rate from 42.74% to 39%.
5. *Higher leave encashment exemption*: The exemption limit for non-government employees has been raised from ₹3 lakhs to ₹25 lakhs, an eight-fold increase.

Starting from FY 2023–24, the new income tax regime has been set as the default option. If you want to continue using the old regime, you must submit the income tax return along with Form 10IEA before the due date. You will have the option to switch between the two regimes annually to check the tax benefits.

Comparison of Tax Rates: Old vs New Regime

Income Slab	Old Tax Regime	New Tax Regime (until 31 March 2023)	New Tax Regime (From 1 April 2023)
₹0–₹2,50,000	–	–	–
₹2,50,000–₹3,00,000	5%	5%	–
₹3,00,000–₹5,00,000	5%	5%	5%
₹5,00,000–₹6,00,000	20%	10%	5%
₹6,00,000–₹7,50,000	20%	10%	10%
₹7,50,000–₹9,00,000	20%	15%	10%
₹9,00,000–₹10,00,000	20%	15%	15%
₹10,00,000–₹12,00,000	30%	20%	15%
₹12,00,000–₹12,50,000	30%	20%	20%
₹12,50,000–₹15,00,000	30%	25%	20%
>₹15,00,000	30%	30%	30%

Additional Surcharge for Women

Women with annual taxable income of more than ₹50 lakhs are required to pay an additional surcharge on top of their income tax slab. The following table lists the surcharges applicable to various income slabs:

Annual Taxable Income	Additional Surcharge Rate
From ₹50 lakh to ₹1 crore	10%
From ₹1 crore to ₹2 crore	15%
Above ₹2 crore	25%

Calculation of Taxable Income for Women

A person's taxable income is calculated based on various types of income, including:

- Salaried income
- Income from business and profession
- Income from capital gains
- Income from other sources such as dividend income, interest earned on fixed deposits, etc.

Understanding these tax slabs, rebates and surcharge rates is essential for women to make informed financial decisions and effectively plan their taxes. One of the exemptions available to women are the basic exemption limit. Women have the same basic exemption limit as men.

Income up to ₹3 lakhs is not taxable. Women above sixty years can avail the senior citizens' exemption, which has a higher limit.

Tax Planning for Different Groups of Women

Entrepreneurs

The rules and regulations for women entrepreneurs are somewhat different from others. If the annual turnover of a woman entrepreneur's business exceeds a particular limit,

GST registration becomes mandatory. Maintaining proper records of invoices and expenses is crucial for availing input tax credit, which can significantly reduce the overall tax liability.

Professionals and Freelancers

If the annual turnover of women working as professionals and freelancers exceeds the prescribed threshold, GST registration is mandatory. Maintaining proper records of services offered and billed is paramount. Further, professionals can avail tax deductions under Section 80C, 80D for health insurance and other relevant sections under the old tax regime.

Corporate Executives

Corporate executives, even though salaried, should be aware of certain GST aspects. Invoices submitted for expense reimbursements should comply with GST regulations to ensure the company can claim input tax credit. Verify that the GSTIN of the company is mentioned on relevant documents for transparent and compliant transactions.

Homemakers

While a housewife may not have direct income, joint investments made with the spouse can contribute to overall tax efficiency for the couple. Certain exemptions and deductions are available for the family, such as those under Section 80C, and these too can contribute to tax optimisation.

Let's consider an example to illustrate the difference between the old and new tax regimes for a salaried woman with an annual income of ₹10,00,000.

The old regime calculation is as follows:

Income Details	Amount (₹)
Gross Income	10,00,000
Less: Standard Deduction	50,000
Less: Section 80C (ELSS)	1,50,000
Less: Section 80D	25,000
Net Taxable Income	7,75,000

The tax liability is calculated based on the old tax regime slabs for ₹7,75,000.

The new regime calculation is as follows:

Income Details	Amount (₹)
Gross Income	10,00,000
Less: Standard Deduction	50,000
Net Taxable Income	9,50,000

The tax liability is calculated based on the new tax regime slabs for ₹9,50,000.

Tax-Effective Investments

Investing in tax-saving instruments such as Public Provident Fund (PPF), equity-linked savings schemes (ELSS), National Pension System (NPS) and tax-saving fixed deposits (FDs) can help reduce taxable income while building wealth.

Understanding the benefits and risks of each investment option is crucial for making informed decisions.

Tax planning is an essential aspect of financial management for women. By understanding the different tax slabs, exemptions and deductions, women can make informed decisions to optimise their tax liability. Whether you are an entrepreneur, professional, corporate executive or homemaker, being aware of tax regulations and planning accordingly can lead to significant financial benefits.

Maximising Tax Benefits: A Guide for Women Taxpayers

'People who complain about taxes can be divided into two classes: men and women.'

—Anonymous

LET'S NOW DELVE INTO THE VARIOUS SECTIONS OF THE INCOME TAX Act that provide benefits and deductions for women, this time looking more into the specifics of the act.

Section 80C Deductions

Section 80C of the Income Tax Act is a powerful tool for tax planning, offering deductions up to ₹1.5 lakhs. Several investment avenues fall under this section:

- *Equity-linked savings scheme (ELSS)*: The ELSS stands out as a versatile investment option, offering both tax benefits under Section 80C and opportunities for wealth creation through equity investments. An ELSS provides an opportunity for substantial tax savings with a lock-in period of three years and potential for higher returns.

- *Public Provident Fund (PPF)*: PPF offers long-term savings with tax advantages under Section 80C. With a tenure of fifteen years, PPF promotes disciplined savings and allows contributions ranging from ₹500 to ₹1.5 lakhs annually. Additionally, it offers loan facilities and partial withdrawals.
- *National Pension System (NPS)*: The NPS combines tax benefits under Section 80C and an additional deduction of up to ₹50,000 under Section 80CCD (1B). It provides investment options in equity, corporate debt and government securities, catering to different risk tolerances and financial goals. The NPS also offers flexibility in withdrawal options at the time of retirement.
- *Tax-saving fixed deposits (FDs)*: A tax-saving FD is a popular investment option that allows individuals and entities to save funds for the future while enjoying tax benefits. Unlike general FD accounts, tax-saving FDs have a lock-in period of five years and offer tax deductions under Section 80C. While the interest earned on the deposit is taxable, tax-saving FDs provide a fixed rate of interest ranging from 5.5% to 7.75%. These FDs offer guaranteed returns and are considered low-risk investments.
- *Employee Provident Fund (EPF)*: Contributions to the EPF are deductible under Section 80C. Contributions are typically deducted from the salary by employers and paid directly to the fund manager.
- *Life insurance premiums*: Premiums paid for life insurance policies covering spouses and children qualify for deductions.

Women can evaluate different policies to ensure both protection and tax benefits.

- *National Savings Certificates (NSC)*: NSCs, with their fixed-income investment option, are eligible for deductions under Section 80C. They are government-initiated saving instruments that come with a tenure of five years and can be easily availed through any post office branch.

By leveraging deductions and exemptions available under various sections of the Income Tax Act, women taxpayers can effectively minimise their tax burden while strategically planning their finances for long-term security and wealth creation.

Here's a quick comparison of the popular tax-saving investment options if your goal is wealth creation too:

Investment Type	Returns	Lock-in Period	Tax on Returns
5-Year Bank Fixed Deposit	5–7%	5 years	Yes
Public Provident Fund (PPF)	7–8%	15 years	No
National Savings Certificate (NSC)	6–8%	5 years	Yes
National Pension System (NPS)	8–10%	Till Retirement	Partially Taxable
ELSS Funds	12–15%	3 years	Tax-Free

ELSS stands out with its dual-benefit—its returns are generally higher and are tax-free. This, coupled with a mere lock-in period of three years, is all the more reason for you to invest in ELSS funds.

Understanding the risk–return profile of each of the investment options discussed allows women to align their choices with their financial goals and risk tolerance. The potential risks and rewards associated with various investment avenues vary, so women can make informed decisions that suit their individual circumstances by learning about each one.

Diversifying investments across different instruments can help reduce the overall risk and enhance the potential for returns. Diversification spreads investment risk across multiple assets, safeguarding against fluctuations in any single asset class.

Finally, when it comes to Section 80C investments with their inherent lock-in periods, a long-term planning approach should be adopted. Women can leverage this lock-in feature to their advantage, using it for disciplined long-term investment and eventual wealth accumulation.

By implementing these strategies, women can take control of their financial futures and make empowered decisions to secure long-term prosperity.

The other available deductions you need to be aware of are listed below.

Health Insurance Benefits (Section 80D)

1. *Deductions for premiums paid*: Section 80D provides deductions for premiums paid towards health insurance policies for self, family and parents.
2. *Preventive health check-up deductions*: Additional deductions are available for the cost of preventive health check-ups, encouraging a proactive approach to healthcare.
3. *Holistic financial planning*: Health insurance not only provides financial security during medical emergencies but also plays a crucial role in holistic financial planning.

Home Loan Benefits (Section 24, 80C and 80EEA)

When taking a home loan, borrowers can avail financial advantages through tax deductions on both the principal and interest components of the loan. These deductions are available under specific sections of the Income Tax Act, such as Section 24 for interest payments and Section 80C for principal repayments. Section 80EEA offers additional deductions on interest for first-time homebuyers, promoting homeownership. Borrowers, including women, can optimise their tax liabilities while promoting homeownership and financial stability by availing these exemptions.

Managing a home loan requires careful financial planning and prudence. By understanding the intricacies of loan structuring, reviewing loan terms regularly and balancing loan repayments with other investments, women can navigate the complexities of home loan management effectively.

By delving into Section 80C deductions, health insurance benefits under Section 80D and the tax efficiency of home loans, women can enhance their knowledge and make informed decisions. This knowledge not only maximises post-tax returns but also contributes to holistic financial well-being and long-term financial security.

Here is the entire list of the various sections and the eligible investment of expense with the threshold of deductions for your quick reference.

Section	Eligible Investment or Expense	Threshold Limit for Deductions
80C	National Savings Certificate	₹1,50,000

Section	Eligible Investment or Expense	Threshold Limit for Deductions
	Public Provident Fund	
	Life insurance premium	
	Repayment of housing loan	
	Tuition fees	
	Sukanya Samridhi Scheme	
	Senior Citizen Saving Scheme	
80CCC	Contribution to specified pension fund	-
80CCD(1)	Contribution towards National Pension scheme (NPS)	
80CCD(1B)	Additional deduction for NPS contribution	₹50,000
80D	Health insurance premium	₹25,000 (self, spouse, children)
	Preventive health scheme	₹50,000 (senior citizens self/parents) ₹5,000 (Preventive health checkup)

Section	Eligible Investment or Expense	Threshold Limit for Deductions
80DD	Medical treatment for differently abled dependent (spouse, children, parents, brother, and sister)	₹75,000 ₹1,25,000 (in case of severe disability)
80DDB	Medical treatment of specified ailment or disease	₹40,000 (for self and dependents) ₹1,00,000 (for senior citizens)
80E	Interest payment of loan taken for higher education	Amount of interest paid
80EEA	Interest paid on loan for residential house	₹1,50,000
80EEB	Interest paid on loan for electrical vehicle	
80G	Donations to eligible charitable and religious institutions, etc.	50% or 100% of the donation
80GG	House rent paid	Whichever is less: - ₹5,000 per month - Rent amount minus 10% of total income - 25% of the total income

Section	Eligible Investment or Expense	Threshold Limit for Deductions
80GGC	Donation made to electoral trust or political party	Amount of donation
80TTA	Saving bank interest	₹10,000
80TTB	Interest on bank deposits received by senior citizens	₹50,000

Beyond Traditional Investments—Special Investment Schemes

In this exploration, we delve into unique investment opportunities specifically tailored for women's financial empowerment, which can supplement standard deductions and schemes available to everyone, thereby becoming advantageous specifically for women.

The *Sukanya Samriddhi Yojana* (SSY) is meticulously crafted to secure the financial future of the girl child, offering attractive interest rates and significant tax benefits. Specifically designed for girl children, this scheme allows a minimum deposit of ₹250 and a maximum of ₹1.5 lakh per financial year. It can be opened in the name of a girl child until she turns ten years old, available at post offices and authorised banks. The SSY permits only one account per girl child and allows partial withdrawals for higher education expenses. The account can be prematurely closed for marriage after the child reaches the age of eighteen, and it matures after twenty-one years from the opening date. This scheme is transferable across India and offers tax benefits under Section 80C, with interest earned being tax-free under Section 10 of the Income

Tax Act. Current interest rate offered is 8.2% (1 January 2024 to 31 June 2024).

By facilitating long-term savings, tax efficiency and secure returns, the SSY ensures funds are readily available for the girl child's education, marriage and future needs.

Similarly, the *Mahila Samman Savings Certificate* (MSSC), introduced as part of Budget 2023, provides women with a distinctive opportunity to earn a fixed interest rate over a two-year period, encouraging savings. Offered by the Government of India, the MSSC carries minimal credit risk and requires a minimum investment of ₹1,000, with investments possible in multiples of ₹100, up to a maximum of ₹2,00,000 per individual. The scheme offers an attractive interest rate of 7.5% per annum, compounded quarterly and credited to the account, with a fixed maturity period of two years from the date of account opening. While investments do not qualify for deductions under Section 80C, the MSSC does not deduct TDS on the interest earned. Multiple accounts can be opened, subject to the total deposit limit and a mandatory three-month gap between subsequent account openings. Nomination facilities are available for up to four nominees per account.

Financial Planning and Investment Strategy

Your choice between PPF, SSY and MSSC should align with your financial goals, whether focused on education planning, marriage expenses or broader savings objectives. Before investing, it is crucial to thoroughly understand each scheme's features, risks and benefits to make informed decisions that align with your financial aspirations. Effective tax planning and continuous reassessment of your financial objectives will empower you to build a secure and prosperous future.

Here's a comparison between MSSC, PPF and SSY.

	Mahila Samman Savings Certificate (MSSC)	Public Provident Fund (PPF)	Sukanya Samriddhi Yojana (SSY)
Eligibility	Women, including minor	Any Indian citizen	Girl child up to 10 years age
Interest Rate	7.50% per annum	7.1% per annum	8% per annum
Deposit Limit	Minimum ₹1,000, Maximum ₹2 lakh	Minimum ₹500, Maximum ₹1.5 lakh	Minimum ₹250, Maximum ₹1.5 lakh
Maturity	2 years	15 years	After 21 years from opening or on marriage at 18 years
Partial Withdrawal	Up to 40% of balance after one year	Up to 50% of balance after seven years	Up to 50% of balance at 18 years for marriage or education
Tax Benefits	No Section 80C	Eligible for deduction under Section 80C	Eligible for deduction under Section 80C

Whether opting for the safety of fixed deposits, exploring the growth potential of mutual funds or leveraging specialised schemes like the SSY and MSSC, you now have the tools to navigate and shape your financial destiny with confidence.

Envisioning Your Retirement: Nominations, Protection and Legacy

'Retirement is not the end of the road. It is the beginning of the open highway.'

—Anonymous

IN OUR EXPLORATION OF RETIREMENT PLANNING AND LEGACY BUILDING, we delve into crucial aspects that shape your financial future and the legacy you leave behind. From strategising for retirement to unravelling the complexities of the Married Women's Property (MWP) Act of 1874, we cover a spectrum of topics aimed at securing your financial well-being.

One fundamental aspect we address is the significance of nominations and wills in estate planning. If you are able to master nominations, your assets will be rightfully transferred to your loved ones, avoiding legal complications and delays.

Nominations are often overlooked as just another formality in financial planning, but they carry significant weight in safeguarding your family's interests. They go beyond paperwork; they serve as a promise to your family that their financial security is your priority, even in your absence.

Furthermore, creating your legacy involves using wills in estate planning. A will is not merely a legal document, it's a blueprint for how your estate should be managed and distributed. Through real-life examples, we highlight how a well-drafted will can provide clarity and peace of mind, ensuring that your assets are distributed according to your wishes.

Mastering Nominations

When you are putting in place nominations, they seem like paperwork. And if they are done right, there is usually no special benefit—your estate goes to your loved ones, as it should be. However, if they are done wrong, things can quickly spiral out of control.

Consider the case of Neha, a dedicated working mother. Neha diligently managed her finances. She invested in a fixed deposit and intended to provide for her daughter's future education. However, she overlooked nominating her daughter as the beneficiary of the deposit. Tragically, Neha passed away unexpectedly, leaving her daughter to deal with not only the emotional loss but also the legal complications and delays surrounding the investment. Her daughter couldn't immediately access the funds, when she really needed them.

Neha's story reminds us that nominations extend beyond a mere checkbox on forms. They are a promise to our loved ones that we've got their back, even in our absence. Nominations ensure that your assets seamlessly transition to the right hands, avoiding legal entanglements and delays.

Single Women and Nominations: A Thoughtful Step

For single women, nominations assume an even greater significance. Maya, a single woman, recognises this and wishes to bequeath part of her property to her niece to support her education. By nominating her niece, Maya ensures that her wish is upheld legally and ethically.

While Rakhi, another single woman living in Mumbai, had no immediate family, she cherished her close friends as her chosen family. She owned various assets and investments that she wanted to pass on to her friends. Rakhi wisely ensured that she nominated her friends as beneficiaries across her investments, bank accounts and insurance policies. This ensured that her assets would reach the right hands without legal entanglements.

Maya's and Rakhi's foresight highlights how nominations can empower single women to shape their legacy. By nominating beneficiaries, they can provide for their loved ones and causes dear to their heart, irrespective of their marital status.

Nominations extend beyond individual accounts and policies—they encompass your family's financial landscape. Regulatory bodies like SEBI and AMFI now mandate nominations for mutual fund investments. This shift places the onus on investors to actively opt out if they wish to forego nominating beneficiaries. This shift reinforces the recognition that nominations are not just a legal formality, but a critical measure for safeguarding your loved ones' interests.

Life is dynamic, and your nominations should mirror this reality. The nominee you choose today may not remain relevant years down the line. To ensure that your intentions align with your current circumstances, review and update your nominations periodically. Moreover, in the unfortunate event of a nominee's demise, it's crucial to verify and update your policies and investments accordingly.

Crafting Your Legacy—Wills and Estate Planning

While nominations hold the key to specific assets, wills offer a holistic blueprint for your entire financial legacy. Think of a will as a heartfelt letter to your family, a guide that articulates your desires for asset distribution, guardianship of minors and more. Importantly, a will remains adaptable through a 'codicil', allowing you to adjust it as life evolves.

Case Study 1: The Consequences of Dying Intestate

Rina, a devoted wife and mother, unexpectedly passed away without leaving a will. The absence of a will meant that Rina's assets, including her family home and savings, were distributed based on legal guidelines rather than her wishes. The heart-wrenching outcome was that her husband and children had to contend with an emotionally taxing legal process during an already challenging time.

Case Study 2: The Power of a Will in Preventing Disputes

Anjali, a woman who wisely recognised the significance of a will, made her intentions clear by nominating her brother as the beneficiary for her insurance policies and bank accounts. However, she took the extra step of drafting a will to ensure that her assets were distributed as she wished. When Anjali passed away unexpectedly, her foresight paid off. Her will took precedence over the nominations, ensuring that her assets reached the intended beneficiaries without any disputes.

The interplay between a will and nominations is crucial to understand. Nominations define the beneficiaries for specific assets, such as insurance policies and bank accounts. However, a will holds the power to override these nominations. For instance, if you've nominated your sister as the beneficiary for an insurance policy, but your will states that the proceeds should go to your children, the will's provisions will prevail. This underlines the importance of creating a comprehensive will to ensure that your final wishes are honoured.

Flexibility and Control: Changing Nominations

Nominations can be altered whenever needed. Whether your circumstances change or you wish to update your beneficiaries, you have the flexibility to modify your nominations. Remember that the provisions of your will ultimately hold precedence over nominations. Also, while you may nominate up to three individuals, it's crucial to specify the exact allocation or share each nominee is entitled to receive. This ensures a smooth transfer of assets and prevents disputes.

Aligning your nominee and beneficiary can offer added clarity and simplicity. When the same person is both the nominee and beneficiary, potential future conflicts are minimised. This approach ensures that your intended beneficiary receives the benefits without potential contention. Taking this thoughtful step prevents ambiguity and safeguards your legacy.

Nominations and wills, when combined, create a robust foundation for your family's financial well-being. While nominations offer precision in asset distribution, a will presents a panoramic view of your estate. By understanding the dynamics of nominations, staying vigilant about updates and appreciating the significance of a will, you display commendable responsibility.

Your dedication to securing your loved ones' financial future is a selfless act transcending time, ensuring a legacy of care.

Action Points

Empowerment begins with action. Here's how you can take charge:

1. *Review your nominations*: Reevaluate your nominations across assets, ensuring alignment with your current intentions.
2. *Understand the will*: Grasp the comprehensive power of a will, the document that encapsulates your entire legacy.
3. *Nominate and will for singles*: Single women, nominate your cherished beneficiaries and craft a will to preserve your legacy.
4. *Have family dialogues*: Initiate conversations about nominations and wills within your family. Though it may be uncomfortable, it is a profound act of care.
5. *Seek professional assistance*: Seek expert guidance to draft a robust, legally sound will that embodies your wishes.

Remember, nominations and wills aren't just legal requirements; they are expressions of love and responsibility. By navigating nominations thoughtfully and comprehending the weight of a will, you are weaving a tapestry of security, transparency and adherence to your values. Your financial legacy stands as a tribute to your unwavering care, ensuring your family's journey remains smooth even in your absence.

As you embark on this journey of financial empowerment and legacy planning, know that your proactive steps today will create a legacy of financial security and compassion for generations to come.

The Married Women's Property Act, 1874 (MWP Act) is a pivotal legislation in safeguarding women's financial interests, especially in the context of life insurance policies.

Meet Anjali, the wife of a successful business owner who meticulously managed various aspects of his enterprise. While he secured loans for his business and had valuable assets and a robust insurance policy, a critical oversight in his personal finances became apparent—he had not endorsed his insurance policy under the MWP Act.

This oversight proved costly when unforeseen circumstances led creditors to seize assets to settle debts, leaving Anjali's family vulnerable. Had they utilised the protective provisions of the MWP Act, the outcome could have been drastically different.

For married policyholders, especially men, endorsing a term insurance plan under the MWP Act ensures that in the event of their demise, the sum assured is exclusively safeguarded for their wife and children. This legal provision shields the insurance proceeds from being claimed by creditors, thus securing the financial future of their family members.

In the realm of women's financial empowerment, the MWP Act serves as a beacon, providing essential protections and ensuring that financial decisions have lasting benefits for families.

Section 5: A Woman's Sovereign Financial Decision

At the heart of the MWP Act, 1874 lies Section 5, a provision that grants married women a remarkable authority: the ability to initiate an insurance policy in their own name, independent of their spouse. This way, women can establish a policy with or without their husband's consent, granting them sole control over the policy's benefits.

Maya, a dedicated homemaker, took a courageous step towards securing her financial independence by investing in a life insurance policy through Section 5 of the MWP Act, 1874. This decision not only ensured her own financial stability but also that of her children, breaking free from financial dependency. Maya's choice exemplifies her empowerment in managing her financial affairs and safeguarding her family's future. By asserting her right to protect her financial interests, Maya paved a path to a more resilient future, where financial security became a cornerstone of their lives.

Section 6: Preserving a Husband's Gift of Security

In Section 6 of the MWP Act, 1874 is a provision that focuses on insurance policies initiated by married men for the benefit of their wives. This provision allows the husband to safeguard his family's financial stability. Under Section 6, the policy remains beyond the control of the husband, creditors or even his estate. This provision effectively gifts financial security, ensuring that a woman's well-being remains shielded from unforeseen circumstances.

Maya, Anjali and many others exemplify how leveraging Sections 5 and 6 of the MWP Act, 1874 can lead to a more secure financial future. Their stories underscore the importance of awareness, action and foresight in achieving financial empowerment. By embracing the spirit of the act, individuals ensure that women's financial interests are protected, providing strength, resilience and enduring security for their families.

Section 6

Navigating Challenges, Empowering Lives

Welcome to the final section of our journey—a pivotal point where challenges become stepping stones, and empowerment ignites a movement. Here, we embark on a journey through diverse landscapes of financial empowerment. From navigating the complexities of finfluencers and risky investments to recognising and overcoming financial abuse, we uncover practical strategies to overcome hurdles and find trusted financial guidance.

Through these insights, we empower ourselves and those who support us, culminating in scripting our own financial success stories. This section isn't just about learning—it's about taking action and becoming teachers of financial empowerment. By creating a ripple effect that starts with us, we empower more lives and pave the way for a future where every woman thrives financially and makes a meaningful difference.

Join us as we embrace this transformative journey to become financially smart women, forging a path of empowerment and setting a powerful example for generations to come.

Navigating the World of Finfluencers and Risky Investments

'Risk comes from not knowing what you're doing.'
—Warren Buffett

HEY THERE, FABULOUS WOMEN! TODAY, WE'RE DIVING INTO A WORLD where financial advice meets the influencer culture—the world of 'finfluencers'. It's like a wild ride with a lot of potential but also some hidden risks. So, grab your favourite beverage, and let's navigate this together, shall we?

In the age of social media, finfluencers are everywhere, dishing out financial advice like confetti. Now, don't get me wrong; some of them genuinely know their stuff and can offer valuable insights. However, it's like a double-edged sword. Many finfluencers might be promoting risky investments, promising quick returns without giving you the full picture of the potential pitfalls.

Quick Returns and Groupthink

When you're scrolling through your feed, you are likely to stumble upon posts or videos promising overnight riches through a specific investment or trading strategy. The catch? These promises often come with hidden risks, and their main goal is to grab attention rather than provide accurate financial advice. Let's be real—sustainable wealth building requires patience, research and a well-thought-out strategy.

The best defence against misleading investment advice? Education, my friend! Take the time to understand different investment options, their associated risks and potential returns. Don't rush into decisions based solely on social media recommendations. Instead, be your own financial guru—conduct thorough research, consult financial professionals and make informed choices that align with your unique financial goals.

Another danger when looking for investment avenues is groupthink. Sometimes, groups of individuals, often formed on social media, come together to collectively invest in stocks or other assets. While collective decision-making can have its advantages, it's crucial to be aware of the risks. Group investments driven by the fear of missing out (FOMO) can lead to impulsive decisions and potential financial losses.

Building a Resilient Mindset

To avoid falling into the herd mentality trap, cultivate a mindset of individual empowerment. Make rational decisions based on your financial goals and risk tolerance. While it's fine to seek advice and learn from others, always remember that your financial journey is as unique as you are. Stay focused on your long-term objectives rather than chasing short-term trends.

Let's dive into a real-life story to bring this home. Aisha, a young woman in her twenties, was enticed by a finfluencer's post about a 'guaranteed' investment promising quick returns. Excited to grow her wealth, she invested a substantial amount without conducting proper research. Unfortunately, the investment turned out to be a scam, so she lost a lot of her money. Aisha learnt the hard way about the importance of due diligence and the risks of being swayed by promises of instant wealth.

While some finfluencers offer valuable insights, many may promote high-risk investments promising quick riches. By staying educated, avoiding a group mentality, exercising caution and discernment and making informed decisions based on your individual financial goals, you can safeguard your financial interests against these risks while benefitting from the wealth of information shared. Remember that building lasting wealth requires careful planning, knowledge and a steady approach that aligns with your financial aspirations.

Cheers to navigating the financial seas like the boss woman you are!

Financial Abuse: Recognising, Overcoming and Thriving

'You are braver than you believe, stronger than you seem, and smarter than you think.'

—A.A. Milne

Let's dive into a topic that might not be the cosiest, but it's one we need to chat about—financial abuse. It's like that sneaky predator that can mess with your life without you even realising it. So, grab a cup of tea, get comfy and let's unveil the mysteries of financial manipulation together.

Step 1: Defining Financial Abuse, the Unseen Shackles

Now, let's start with the basics.

What's financial abuse? It's like those unseen shackles that mess with your money and, in turn, your life. It's not just about dollar signs; it's about control and manipulation that can seep into every aspect of your world.

At its core, financial abuse involves a range of tactics designed to exploit and control, reaching far beyond the realms of monetary transactions. It's like being caught in unseen shackles, restrained by the manipulation of your economic resources. This can range from controlling access to bank accounts to coercing victims into surrendering their hard-earned money.

And why on earth do people do this? Well, it's a bit like a power trip. Financial control becomes a tool for some folks to establish dominance. It's like they're saying, 'Look at me, I've got the purse strings, and I'm in charge.' It often stems from a deep-seated need for dominance within a relationship. It can be a manifestation of insecurities or a desire for superiority. By exploring these motives, we're laying the groundwork for awareness and resilience.

So, understanding this twisted reasoning is our first step to breaking free. It requires shedding light on these subtle yet powerful methods so you can identify the signs before things get too tangled.

Financial abuse is present in 99% of domestic violence cases, demonstrating its widespread use as a method of entrapment.[7]

Step 2: Recognising the Shadows

Let's equip ourselves with the tools to spot those early warning signs, the subtle shadows that precede the overt manifestations of control. Navigating these red flags is pivotal in preventing the escalation of financial abuse.

---

7 Sherri Gordon, 'How to Identify Financial Abuse in a Relationship', Verywell Mind, 29 November 2022, https://www.verywellmind.com/financial-abuse-4155224.

Recognising the early signs is like deciphering a code that operates in the shadows of everyday interactions. Watch out for things like being isolated from financial information, feeling financially dependent or suddenly having someone else taking over control of your resources.

Real-life stories of women who have experienced financial abuse highlight this issue. The prevalence of matrimonial fraud is a global concern, with significant numbers reported both in India and worldwide.

This alarming trend is part of a larger issue that extends beyond India. In Mumbai alone, there have been sixty-two cases of matrimonial fraud between 2021 and May 2024, with only fifteen successfully resolved.[8]

The documentary series on Prime Video and Amazon MGM Studios *#WeddingCon* is another eye-opener. It features five women who share their harrowing experiences of being deceived by men. Their stories highlight the prevalence of mental, physical and financial abuse, often realised too late. Everyone, especially women, should watch this to stay aware and alert.

Financial abuse often affects women who have money but fall victim to manipulation by partners, siblings and even their own children.

---

8 Vinay Dalvi, 'Matrimonial frauds: Mumbai police warns prospective brides and grooms', *Hindustan Times*, 20 February 2022, https://www.hindustantimes.com/cities/mumbai-news/matrimonial-frauds-mumbai-police-warns-prospective-brides-and-grooms-101645366696883.html; Vijay Kumar Yadav, 'Matrimonial fraud: Mumbai woman falls into business trap of 'groom', loses Rs 55 lakh', *The Indian Express*, 26 June 2024, https://indianexpress.com/article/cities/mumbai/matrimonial-fraud-mumbai-woman-business-trap-9416193/.

Let me share with you some real-life stories of women who have experienced financial abuse sometimes knowingly and always feeling like a victim while sometimes getting unknowingly sucked into it and falling into the trap.

Maya's Dilemma: Eroding Independence for Security

Maya, a talented artist, had dreams as vibrant as her canvases. When she got married, her partner seemed supportive, encouraging her artistic pursuits. However, as time passed, a subtle shift occurred. He insisted she quit her job, assuring her that he would manage their finances to provide security. Trusting his intentions, she handed over her earnings.

As the days unfolded, the promise of security morphed into a stifling control. He began dictating every aspect of their financial life, from budgeting to investments. Isolation followed; Maya found herself cut off from financial information and discussions. Her independence eroded, replaced by a suffocating dependency.

In Maya's case, the manipulation started with seemingly reasonable requests. Maintaining financial independence is essential for every individual, so be wary of surrendering control over earnings. Open communication about financial decisions is key.

Neha's Deception: Love Turned to Exploitation

Neha's love story read like a fairy tale, a whirlwind romance with her college sweetheart promising a future of shared dreams and prosperity. Entranced by his charm, she trusted him implicitly, believing in their mutual vision for a blissful life together.

But beneath the veneer of love and devotion lurked a sinister truth. Neha's husband, once the epitome of affection and support, gradually revealed his deceitful nature. He cunningly persuaded Neha to sell her cherished property, promising a brighter future built on their combined resources.

However, as time passed, Neha began to notice subtle signs of financial strain. Small discrepancies in their accounts, unexplained expenses and secretive behaviours hinted at a troubling hidden reality.

The façade of marital bliss shattered when Neha uncovered the truth about her husband's clandestine spending habits. Behind closed doors, he was squandering their savings on extravagant purchases, luxurious vacations and risky investments. His reckless disregard for their financial well-being plunged them into a downward spiral of debt and uncertainty.

Caught in a web of lies and betrayal, Neha was left to bear the burden of their financial woes alone. The dreams they had nurtured together turned to dust, replaced by the harsh reality of exploitation and deceit.

Neha's story serves as a stark reminder of the importance of transparency and joint decision-making in relationships. Trust, once broken, is difficult to mend. Partners must be vigilant and actively involved in financial matters to prevent exploitation and protect their shared future.

Siblings' Strife: Family Bonds and Financial Control

Anu and Riya shared more than just a family bond; they shared trust, empathy and a lifetime of shared experiences. Riya, however, saw an opportunity to manipulate this bond for her own gain, constantly borrowing money from Anu under the pretext of urgent needs. Riya's requests grew more frequent, fuelling frivolous expenses.

As Anu, driven by empathy and familial duty, continued to lend, she found herself strained and drained, both emotionally and financially. Riya's manipulation not only strained their relationship but also left Anu questioning the boundaries of familial responsibility.

The case of Anu and Riya highlights how financial abuse can extend beyond romantic relationships to familial bonds. It underscores the importance of setting boundaries, even within families, and being vigilant against manipulation, as trust should not be exploited.

Ananya's Struggle—A Single Mother Navigating Financial Abuse

Meet Ananya, a resilient single mother whose life revolved around her only son, Aarav. Ananya, holding down a job and standing on the brink of retirement, faced the dual challenges of financial strain and declining health. As she battled anxiety and major health issues, her vulnerability became an unwitting target for her son's manipulation.

A dedicated single mother, she shouldered the responsibility of being the sole breadwinner for her family. Her job, once a source of stability, had become a lifeline for both her and Aarav. As she approached retirement, the prospect of relying on a fixed income added an extra layer of stress to her financial situation.

Apart from the financial challenges, Ananya grappled with her own health issues and anxiety. The burden of being the sole provider, compounded by her declining health, created a perfect storm of vulnerability. Aarav, aware of his mother's struggles, seized the opportunity to exploit her emotional and financial state.

Aarav's requests for financial assistance weren't just about needs anymore; they were about wants. In the guise of securing a better future, he urged his mother to dip into her savings and retirement funds. Ananya, haunted by the fear of burdening her son with her health expenses, succumbed to the emotional manipulation.

The cycle of giving accelerated as Aarav became adept at using Ananya's anxiety and health concerns against her. The financial drain not only endangered Ananya's present stability but also threatened the security of her retirement years.

Ananya's heart was torn between the responsibility she felt towards her son and the realisation that the financial strain was jeopardising her own well-being. The anxiety she battled became a silent accomplice to Aarav's emotional manipulation.

Despite recognising the unsustainable path they were on, Ananya felt trapped by a sense of maternal duty and the fear of worsening her health condition. The weight of responsibility, both financial and emotional, pressed down on her like an insurmountable burden.

Ananya's narrative underscores the unique challenges faced by single mothers who, in their dedication, may inadvertently become targets of financial abuse. It emphasises the importance of establishing clear boundaries and recognising when the line between support and manipulation is crossed.

For readers, Ananya's story serves as a poignant reminder of the need to safeguard one's financial future, especially when nearing retirement or facing health issues. It encourages a thoughtful examination of relationships and a proactive approach to addressing financial concerns.

As we conclude this section, remember that awareness is the first step to breaking free from the shadows of financial manipulation. By recognising, overcoming and thriving beyond these challenges, you possess the strength to reclaim autonomy and create a life filled with empowerment and financial well-being.

Step 3: Resilience and Revival

The next crucial step is fostering resilience and revival. These two pillars are instrumental in guiding survivors towards healing and growth, helping them reclaim their lives. Breaking free from the clutches of financial abuse requires not only recognition and understanding but also a comprehensive strategy for recovery.

Breaking free from financial abuse is not a solitary journey; it requires a network of trust and support. A supportive community aids survivors in their journey towards healing. Allies on the road to recovery can come in various forms, including friends, family, support groups or professionals specialising in domestic abuse.[9]

Survivors are encouraged to reach out, share their experiences and lean on the strength of those who genuinely care. Building a support ecosystem is about breaking the isolation that often accompanies financial abuse, fostering connections that provide emotional sustenance and seeking practical guidance. It's essential for survivors to identify and confide in trustworthy individuals who can offer empathy and understanding. Establishing a robust support network is a foundational step

---

9 For helplines, visit the National Commission for Women website: http://www.ncw.nic.in/helplines.

towards reclaiming one's life and moving beyond the shadows of financial manipulation.

Reclaiming financial independence is inseparable from the process of healing emotional scars. We'll now look at resources, from counselling services to specialised apps, to aid survivors in navigating their emotional healing process.

Survivors are encouraged to seek professional help to tackle the profound impact of financial abuse on mental and emotional well-being. Trained counsellors and therapists can provide a safe space to process trauma, explore coping mechanisms and develop strategies for rebuilding self-esteem.

Moreover, self-help tools, such as meditation apps and mental health resources, can complement formal therapy, allowing survivors to engage in daily practices that nurture their mental and emotional well-being. Healing is an integral part of the journey towards empowerment, and survivors are encouraged to prioritise their mental health as they navigate the path to recovery.

Empowerment against financial manipulation begins with knowledge. We will now see the resources available, including online tools and community-based financial education, empowering them to make informed decisions about their financial future.

Financial literacy acts as a shield against manipulation. Survivors are encouraged to learn about budgeting, investing and managing their finances on their own. Online platforms, workshops and community resources provide accessible avenues for acquiring financial knowledge. By gaining financial wisdom, survivors not only break free from the cycle of manipulation but also acquire the tools to make informed choices, fostering a sense of control and autonomy over their financial destinies.

Empowerment doesn't end with escaping abuse; it's about seizing control of one's narrative. After facing abuse, rebuilding your life is crucial, from setting financial goals to embracing new opportunities and cultivating resilience. It involves setting achievable financial goals, whether it's building an emergency fund, pursuing education or starting a new career.

Survivors are encouraged to envision a future beyond the shadows, where they are the architects of their destiny. Survivors are urged to embrace new opportunities, discover their passions and rebuild their lives with newfound strength and determination. The steps we have discussed serve as a roadmap for those ready to move beyond survival and embrace a future filled with possibilities.

Awareness is the catalyst for change in the realm of financial abuse. By unveiling its signs, fostering support networks and promoting financial education, we embark on a journey to eradicate financial manipulation. Survivors possess the strength to rise from adversity, reclaim their autonomy and achieve empowerment in every facet of their lives.

I've tried to write this chapter as if we're having a meaningful conversation. I hope it feels like you're chatting with a knowledgeable friend because you deserve nothing less. By recognising, overcoming and thriving beyond the challenges posed by financial abuse, you can pave the path to empowerment and reclaim control over your lives.

CHAPTER 3

Overcoming Financial Hurdles: Staying Informed and Vigilant

'The best way to predict the future is to create it.'

—Peter Drucker

OVERCOMING FINANCIAL HURDLES REQUIRES BOTH AWARENESS AND adaptability. We need to recognise common financial pitfalls and arm ourselves with knowledge against them. Once we embrace the power of adaptation, we learn to stay informed, adjust to changes and cultivate a proactive approach to secure our financial future. Join us as we explore the strategies and insights needed to conquer obstacles and achieve financial success.

Step 1: Recognising Financial Pitfalls—Common Obstacles

Financial empowerment is not just about setting goals and making investments; it is also about recognising the potential

242

pitfalls that can hinder your progress. Listed below are some of the common pitfalls we tend to encounter.

Obstacle 1—Overspending and Debt Accumulation

Maya, a dynamic and career-oriented woman, found herself caught in the allure of instant gratification. Her love for shopping and dining out became more than just occasional indulgences and evolved into habits that began to overshadow her financial prudence.

Initially, Maya's spending sprees were manageable, a small treat here and there amidst her busy schedules. However, as time passed, these indulgences grew more frequent and extravagant. Maya found herself swiping her credit card with increasing frequency, lured by the promise of convenience and immediate satisfaction.

As the months went by, Maya's credit card bills began to pile up, each statement revealing a mounting debt that seemed to grow larger with every passing cycle. Despite her initial attempts to rationalise her spending and reassure herself that she could manage the payments, Maya soon found herself trapped in what felt like insurmountable debt.

Facing the reality of her financial situation, Maya was filled with a sense of anxiety and frustration. The burden of her mounting debt weighed heavily on her, casting a shadow over her aspirations and goals. Each credit card bill was a stark reminder of her overspending and its consequences.

However, Maya refused to succumb to despair. Realising that she needed to take decisive action to break free from debt, she sat down seriously for some financial introspection and was determined to be more disciplined. With determination and perseverance, Maya devised a comprehensive plan to tackle her debt, prioritising repayment and curbing her spending habits.

Maya's path to financial freedom was not easy. It required sacrifices and restraint, as well as a willingness to confront her spending habits head-on. She took proactive steps to reduce her expenses, cutting back on non-essential purchases and redirecting her focus towards building a more secure financial future.

Slowly but steadily, Maya began to make progress. With each payment she made, she felt a sense of empowerment and liberation, knowing that she was taking control of her financial destiny. Over time, Maya emerged from the shadow of debt, reclaiming her financial independence and laying the groundwork for a brighter future.

Maya's journey is a powerful reminder of the dangers of overspending and the importance of financial discipline. By confronting her financial challenges head-on and adopting a proactive mindset, Maya was able to overcome adversity and pave the way for a more secure and prosperous future.

Avoid falling into the trap of overspending and debt by following these steps:

1. *Budgeting*: Create a realistic budget that outlines your income, expenses and savings goals. Stick to this budget to avoid unnecessary expenditures.

2. *Emergency fund*: Build an emergency fund that covers three to six months' worth of living expenses. This safety net can help you avoid resorting to high-interest debt in times of crisis.

3. *Debt management*: If you have existing debts, prioritise paying off high-interest debts first. Consider consolidating loans or seeking professional advice if needed.

Obstacle 2—Inadequate Emergency Planning

Priya, a diligent professional, believed her stable job was enough to secure her financial future. However, an unexpected medical emergency left her struggling to cover hefty medical bills. She was entirely dependent on the group medical insurance provided by her company, which proved to be insufficient for the expenses she faced. Consequently, she had to dip into her savings to pay these bills.

Priya's experience highlights the importance of preparing for unforeseen events and having a safety net in place.

Ensure you are ready for unexpected emergencies by considering these steps:

1. *Emergency fund*: Set up an emergency fund that covers your essential expenses in case of unexpected job loss, medical expenses or other unforeseen situations.
2. *Insurance coverage*: Invest in health, life and disability insurance to protect yourself and your family from financial shocks.
3. *Diversify income*: Explore side hustles or alternative income sources to bolster your financial stability and reduce reliance on a single income stream.

Obstacle 3—Neglecting Retirement Planning

Rashmi, a driven professional in her thirties, was immersed in the hustle and bustle of her career. With demanding deadlines and responsibilities, she hardly found time to pause and consider her long-term financial well-being. Retirement planning seemed like a distant concern, something she could address later when she had more time and resources at her disposal.

Despite earning a decent income, Rashmi's focus was primarily on meeting her immediate financial needs and enjoying her present lifestyle. She allocated her earnings towards rent, bills, occasional indulgences and building an emergency fund, but retirement planning never made it to the top of her priority list.

As years passed by, Rashmi's perception of time began to shift. She started to realise the significance of retirement planning and the need to secure her financial future. However, by then, she found herself playing catch-up, facing the daunting task of accumulating enough savings to retire comfortably.

Rashmi's journey highlights a common pitfall among many individuals—neglecting retirement planning in the belief that there is plenty of time ahead. However, as time waits for no one, Rashmi's realisation serves as a wake-up call to take proactive steps towards securing one's retirement, regardless of age or current financial situation.

To secure your retirement years, take these steps:

1. *Start early*: Begin saving for retirement as early as possible. The power of compounding can significantly impact your retirement savings over time.

2. *Retirement accounts*: Contribute to retirement accounts like EPF and NPS to take advantage of tax benefits and employer contributions and invest in mutual funds for the long term with a proper retirement strategy plan (a professional financial coach or advisor can guide you in this).

3. *Regular review*: Regularly assess your retirement plan and adjust contributions based on your changing circumstances and financial goals.

Obstacle 4—Lack of Investment Knowledge

Neha, a diligent professional with a stable income, always harboured the desire to invest and grow her wealth. However, she found herself hesitating to begin because she felt she didn't understand financial markets. The jargon-filled language and complex concepts seemed daunting, leaving Neha feeling overwhelmed and uncertain about where to begin.

As a result, Neha kept her savings parked in traditional savings accounts, earning minimal interest, and barely keeping up with inflation. While she understood the importance of investing for the future, the fear of making uninformed decisions held her back from exploring potential opportunities in the market.

Neha's reluctance to invest not only stagnated her financial growth but also limited her ability to build wealth over time. Without the knowledge and confidence to navigate the investment landscape, Neha remained stuck in a cycle of missed opportunities and underutilised resources.

Neha's situation highlights the importance of financial education and empowerment. By acquiring the necessary knowledge and skills to understand investment options and strategies, individuals like Neha can overcome their fears and make informed decisions to achieve their financial goals.

Overcome the barrier of inadequate investment knowledge:

1. *Educate yourself*: Take the time to learn about different investment options, risk management and long-term wealth-building strategies.
2. *Seek professional guidance*: Consult a certified financial advisor to create a personalised investment plan aligned with your goals and risk tolerance.

3. *Start small*: Begin with simple investments like mutual funds or index funds, gradually expanding your portfolio as you gain confidence.

Recognising financial pitfalls is the first step towards securing your financial future. By staying vigilant and proactive, you can arm yourself with the knowledge needed to navigate these obstacles successfully. The stories of Maya, Priya, Rashmi and Neha remind us that with awareness, education and strategic planning, you can overcome challenges and achieve your financial aspirations.

Action Points

1. *Self-assessment*: Reflect on your financial habits and identify potential pitfalls that could hinder your progress.
2. *Education*: Invest time in learning about personal finance, budgeting, debt management, investing and retirement planning.
3. *Strategic planning*: Develop a comprehensive financial plan that addresses your short-term and long-term goals, emergency fund, insurance coverage and retirement savings.

Money impacts every facet of life, from where you live to the vacations you take. Charting your financial course begins with a dialogue, a conversation with your immediate family and everyone intimately linked to you financially that transcends fear and fosters understanding.

Initiating a candid and fearless conversation about your financial journey is the cornerstone of a robust and healthy partnership.

Here are three empowering questions every couple should delve into:

- *Lay the financial cards on the table*: Take a deep dive into the numbers, laying out your income, debts and the intricate details of your bank accounts. This transparent discussion sets the stage for financial clarity and joint decision-making.
- *Craft your empowered financial vision*: Envision your shared financial future with clarity and purpose. What are your joint goals and aspirations? Define your empowered and rich life, ensuring that your financial journey aligns seamlessly with your collective dreams.
- *Unveil your money histories*: Peel back the layers of your money stories. Understand each other's upbringing with money—the values, beliefs and learnt behaviours. Unravelling these threads provides insights into your financial dynamics and fosters a deeper connection on this crucial journey.

Embarking on your financial life together requires courage, openness and a shared vision. These three pivotal points pave the way for a foundation built on trust, understanding and the collective pursuit of a financially empowered future.

Step 2: The Power of Adaptation—Navigating Change

In a rapidly changing world, the capacity to adapt and remain well-informed is paramount for securing your financial future. As you navigate the intricate landscape of finances, adaptability and a proactive approach can lead to resilience and flexibility.

Let's delve into financial intelligence and its pivotal role in ensuring your economic well-being.

Financial acumen goes beyond the mere accumulation of wealth; it's about making informed decisions, practising prudent financial management and erecting a solid bedrock of financial resilience. These principles empower you to face life's unforeseen challenges with poise and assurance, enabling you to maintain your financial trajectory.

At the core of financial intelligence lies one principle: don't allocate more than two-thirds of your income towards your expenditures. This cardinal guideline serves as a blueprint for establishing a firm financial base. It ensures you create a safety net that not only provides security but also grants you the flexibility to seize emerging opportunities.

Frugality is often misinterpreted as austerity, yet it embodies mindful spending. It entails optimising your resources, eradicating wasteful habits and channelling funds into endeavours that align with your long-term goals. Practising frugality fosters a profound appreciation for the value of money and its potential to shape your financial trajectory over time.

Another fundamental aspect of financial intelligence is acknowledging the ripple effect of every decision you make. Informed choices, both in financial matters and in your personal life, become a pillar of resilience. Through financial literacy, you gain the skills to understand investments, savings strategies and long-term planning, such that you can make decisions that lead to enduring prosperity.

Life is full of unexpected challenges. By combining adaptability and resilience, highlighted by having choices and being flexible, you can tackle these challenges and come out stronger. This approach isn't just about money—it also applies to your mental and emotional strength, giving you the confidence to handle tough times.

The principles of financial intelligence pave the way for embracing choices without hesitation. These choices span from entrepreneurial pursuits to career transitions and pivotal life decisions. A robust financial foundation, fortified by the discussed principles, liberates you to chase your aspirations with conviction, unburdened by the uncertainties often tied to financial struggles.

Navigating Change with Confidence

In a world brimming with financial uncertainties, the journey towards financial intelligence is a beacon of hope. Flexibility empowers you not only with financial prudence but also with a heightened quality of life. Every decision, regardless of its magnitude, contributes to your eventual prosperity.

As you traverse this path, you will discover that financial intelligence enables you to sculpt a future full of resilience, freedom and fulfilment. Armed with the SMARTER approach and the concept of money management, you possess the tools to navigate the complexities of finance and pave the path to your desired financial future.

The SMARTER Way to Wealth and the Six Money Management Buckets

The SMARTER approach to wealth management is defined as follows:

- **S**: Saving—Construct a robust savings plan.

- **M**: Money management skills—Cultivate skills for effective financial management.
- **A**: Attitude—Foster a positive and proactive financial mindset.
- **R**: Resources—Employ available resources judiciously.
- **T**: Time—Grasp the potency of compounding over time.
- **E**: Equity—Diversify investments for growth.
- **R**: Review—Regularly evaluate and adapt your financial strategies.

Remember, the SMARTER way is always available at your fingertips, guiding you towards a financially secure future.

The Six Buckets for Money Management[10] are concepts we are visited earlier:

1. *Emergency fund*: Reserve for unforeseen expenses.
2. *Short-term goals*: Funds for upcoming endeavours.
3. *Long-term goals*: Savings and investments for substantial aims.
4. *Investments*: Diversify for sustained wealth growth.
5. *Debt repayment*: Allocate resources to reduce debts.
6. *Charitable contributions*: Set aside for philanthropic pursuits.

---

10 This concept is inspired from the book by T. Harv Eker, *Secrets of the Millionaire Mind: Mastering the Inner Game of Wealth* (HarperCollins, 2007).

CHAPTER 4

Finding Your Financial Guide

'A mentor is someone who sees more talent and ability within you than you see in yourself, and helps bring it out of you.'
—Bob Proctor

DR DIPALI AND DR ANAND SHARMA, A HIGHLY ACCOMPLISHED married couple in the medical field, have a fascinating story of how they navigate the intricate landscape of personal finance, involving their childhood experiences and emotional nuances.

The professional success of this dynamic duo positioned them to embark on the journey of homeownership. Despite having the means to comfortably buy a home, a subtle reluctance lingered in their discussions about taking a home loan.

As our conversations unfolded, it became evident that Dr Anand's reservations were deeply rooted in the financial struggles of his childhood. The money problems his family faced when he was a child left an indelible mark on him, making the idea of a loan seem like a burden rather than a strategic financial tool.

On the other hand, Dr Dipali's hesitance stemmed from family anecdotes and societal whispers, in which loans were always shown as being shackles rather than pathways to financial growth. These shared childhood experiences, although unspoken, significantly shaped their financial decisions.

In their counselling sessions, we delved into the multiple emotional layers that created this reluctance in the couple. Creating a space for open conversations allowed them to articulate their fears and explore the emotional undercurrents influencing their financial decisions.

Once they realised that their financial journey was intertwined with their emotions, we were able to tailor a comprehensive plan to overcome the problem. This wasn't just about numbers; it was about acknowledging and integrating the emotional nuances that influenced their decision-making. The goal was to transform scepticism into informed choices that resonated with their aspirations.

The journey wasn't without its challenges, but Dr Dipali and Dr Anand's commitment to overcoming their fears led them to have a more empowered financial outlook. Regular reviews, updates on market dynamics and proactive communication ensured they remained not just informed but also confident in their financial choices.

As time progressed, a shift occurred in the couple's perception. The home loan, once viewed with scepticism, became a strategic instrument for wealth creation. They eventually realised that their childhood fears need not dictate their financial present or future—they could leverage a home loan to not only buy a house but also optimise their wealth.

The doctors' story underscores the transformative power of acknowledging the emotional baggage that often shapes financial decisions. By unravelling the layers of scepticism and fear, individuals can pave the way for informed, strategic choices that align with their unique financial goals.

Dr Dipali and Dr Anand's journey illustrates the profound connection between emotions and finances where awareness is the key to unlocking a path towards financial empowerment. Their transformative experience with their financial advisor shows how the right guidance can untangle the emotional threads that often hinder sound financial decision-making. Personal finance is indeed a journey as unique and nuanced as everyone's personal history.

The Quest for Guidance: Choosing a Financial Coach

As Dr Dipali and Dr Anand decided to address their financial concerns, they realised that they needed a seasoned financial coach by their side. Selecting the right coach became a crucial step, akin to finding a trustworthy compass for their financial voyage. Here are some characteristics to watch out for when selecting your coach.

Credentials and Qualifications

Their search led them to a financial coach with recognised credentials and qualifications, which assured them that their guide had the necessary expertise to navigate the intricate financial landscape. The Certified Financial Planner (CFP) certification and the Chartered Financial Analyst (CFA) certification were two indicators of the coach's competence.

Industry Experience

Dr Dipali and Dr Anand understood the significance of experience in the ever-evolving financial world. They sought a coach with a proven track record, someone who had weathered market fluctuations and economic shifts. This experience instilled confidence that their coach could provide insights based on a nuanced understanding of real-world financial dynamics.

Client Testimonials and Referrals

The couple were meticulous in researching client testimonials and seeking referrals before making a final choice. Positive reviews from individuals with similar financial goals and challenges became guiding lights, pointing them towards a coach who had successfully guided others on similar journeys.

The Role of a Financial Coach: Beyond Numbers

The doctors' chosen financial coach played a pivotal role in reshaping not only their financial strategies but also their mindset. The coach's impact went beyond spreadsheets and investments; it addressed their unique fears and aspirations.

Unravelling Emotional Baggage

The coach initiated candid conversations, creating a safe space for Dr Dipali and Dr Anand to articulate their fears and past experiences. By unravelling the emotional baggage, the coach addressed the root causes of scepticism and hesitation, laying the foundation for a more rational and informed financial approach.

Tailored Financial Planning

Recognising that personal finance is a deeply personal journey, the coach crafted a personalised financial plan. This plan not only considered the numerical aspects of wealth creation but also integrated the emotional nuances unique to Dr Dipali and Dr Anand. It became a roadmap that resonated with their aspirations and values.

Continuous Guidance and Education

The financial coach understood the importance of continuous education and guidance. Regular reviews, updates on market trends and proactive communication ensured that Dr Dipali and Dr Anand remained informed and empowered. This ongoing support was instrumental in helping them make smart and informed decisions.

The Epiphany

As Dr Dipali and Dr Anand progressed on their financial journey, a profound shift occurred. The coach's guidance transformed scepticism into confidence and fear into empowerment. They began to see that personal finance wasn't just about managing money; it was about managing emotions, making informed choices and aligning their financial decisions with their unique life goals.

This story highlights the transformative power of a qualified and experienced financial coach, who not only guides in matters of wealth but also understands the individual behind the numbers.

Even the Best Have Coaches

Think about legends like Sachin Tendulkar, Serena Williams, Roger Federer and Virat Kohli. Despite their immense talent and natural ability, they all had coaches who played pivotal roles in their careers. A coach helps bring out the best in you and accelerates your progress, ensuring you don't have to reinvent the wheel. They keep you focused on your goals, prevent distractions and help you avoid the temptation of 'shiny objects' that can divert your attention from what truly matters.

The work done by a financial coach reiterates that, usually, personal finance is about *personal* things than just about *finance*. Each person's financial story is a mosaic of experiences, fears and aspirations. It's a journey that can be fraught with costly mistakes when emotions and unconscious mindsets take the reins. An experienced financial coach becomes a trusted guide, mentor and ally, helping you navigate the complexities of your financial landscape, make smart and informed decisions and ultimately ensure that no one, not even your own fears, stands in the way of your goals.

Empowering the Future: A Mother's Guide to Cultivating Financial Wisdom in Children

'The best way to teach your kids about taxes is by eating 30% of their ice cream.'

—Bill Murray

IN THE BUSTLING HOUSEHOLD OF MRS MEHTA, A MOTHER OF TWO young daughters, financial empowerment began in a thoughtful and intentional manner. Recognising the crucial role mothers play in shaping their children's financial mindsets, Mrs Mehta embarked on a mission to instil healthy money habits in her girls.

As open communication had great power in fostering financial awareness, Mrs Mehta initiated conversations about money over cosy dinners and weekend gatherings, sharing age-appropriate insights with her daughters. From the basics of earning and spending to the more nuanced concepts of saving and investing, these discussions became a cornerstone of their family dynamics.

Mrs Mehta encouraged her daughters to take on small responsibilities within the household so that their financial education went beyond theory into practice. From creating the grocery list to comparing prices at the supermarket, the girls became active participants in financial decision-making.

To make the grocery shopping experience engaging, Mrs Mehta introduced a reward system. The girls earned points for helping create the list, finding discounts and making responsible choices. These points were later converted into a small allowance or treats, instilling the concept of earning and enjoying the rewards of thoughtful decision-making.

One summer, Mrs Mehta involved her daughters in planning the family vacation. Together, they created a budget, allocating funds for accommodation, travel and activities. This hands-on experience not only taught the girls about financial planning but gave them a sense of responsibility as they actively contributed to decisions that impacted the family's finances.

Together, they set up automated savings accounts, teaching the girls the value of consistency and delayed gratification. Mrs Mehta used simple language and relatable examples to demystify the world of finances for her young learners.

Mrs Mehta introduced her daughters to our unique S.M.A.R.T.E.R Way to Wealth acronym and our SMART Life Automated Accounting System.

A portion of their allowance automatically went into different 'accounts'—one for short-term goals like toys and treats, another for long-term goals like education or a dream vacation. This practical approach not only made saving tangible but also was an example of goal-oriented financial planning.

The Power of Early Financial Literacy

Mrs Mehta's commitment to nurturing financial literacy in her daughters bore fruit as they grew older. The girls, now teenagers, exhibited a natural inclination towards responsible financial behaviour. From making informed choices about extracurricular activities to understanding the importance of budgeting for personal expenses, the seeds of financial wisdom sown in childhood had flourished.

As teenagers, inspired by their mother's approach, the girls started a small business of their own. The lessons about budgeting, saving and investing were put into practice as they managed their earnings and expenses, gaining practical insights that would serve them well into adulthood.

Mothers can have a transformative impact on shaping their children's financial futures. By fostering open conversations, involving children in financial decisions and introducing practical experiences, they become architects of a legacy that extends far beyond dollars and cents.

The takeaway from Mrs Mehta's story is clear: a mother's guidance is a powerful force in cultivating financial wisdom in the next generation. By embracing these principles, mothers can contribute not only to their children's financial knowledge but also to the development of healthy and wealthy habits that will serve them well throughout their lives. If Mrs Mehta could do it, so could you as you have completely absorbed all that is needed to be a financially smart woman.

Empowering Your Domestic Staff Financially

'No one has ever become poor by giving.'

—Anne Frank

IN TODAY'S FAST-PACED WORLD, FINANCIAL LITERACY IS A VITAL TOOL for securing our own future and uplifting those who support us daily. This chapter is a roadmap for women to empower their domestic staff, providing them with the essential tools and knowledge for financial security and prosperity.

This is not only a gesture of kindness but also a smart investment in our own well-being. When our domestic staff are financially secure, they are better equipped to perform their duties effectively and with peace of mind. This can lead to a more harmonious and productive work environment, benefitting both employers and employees alike.

Moreover, these measures foster a sense of loyalty and trust in the employer–employee relationship. When employees feel valued and supported, they are more likely to be loyal to their employers and go above and beyond in their roles. This can lead to higher job satisfaction, lower turnover rates and, ultimately, a more stable and successful household or workplace.

Furthermore, empowering our domestic staff financially contributes to breaking the cycle of poverty and promoting social mobility. By providing them with access to financial education and resources, we give them the tools they need to improve their economic situation and pursue their goals. This not only transforms their lives but also has a ripple effect on their families and communities, fostering greater prosperity and opportunity for all.

This way, we contribute to building a more inclusive and equitable society. Financial empowerment is a fundamental human right, and by ensuring that all members of our society have access to the resources they need to thrive, we create a more just and compassionate world for everyone.

Overall, empowering our domestic staff financially is not just a moral imperative but also a strategic investment in our collective future. By sharing the tools, knowledge and resources that they need to achieve financial security and prosperity, we create a more resilient, productive and inclusive society for generations to come.

So, let's work together to make a meaningful difference.

Initiating conversations and building trust: Begin by initiating conversations about financial planning in a comfortable setting. Share your own journey and experiences with money management. Establishing trust is crucial in this process.

For example, over a cup of tea, casually mention how setting aside a small portion of earnings each month for investment has helped you achieve some of your long-term goals. You can then go on to suggest that they should also adopt a similar strategy, helping them divide their income into expenses and savings.

Education on essential financial tools: Introduce them to basic financial tools such as government insurance schemes (PMSBY and PMJJBY). Explain the benefits of these schemes in simple language, highlighting their role as a safety net in unforeseen circumstances. You may sometimes even need to begin right from asking them if they have a bank account of their own and how they should go about getting one for themselves.

Share a story or anecdote about someone who benefitted from an insurance scheme during a tough time. Explain how these schemes can provide financial support in similar situations. The stories discussed in this book can also be quoted, if you can't think of any specific example.

Guidance on investment opportunities: Start with the basics of saving and gradually introduce them to the concept of mutual funds and systematic investment planning (SIP). Use relatable examples to illustrate how even small investments can grow substantially over time. You may also need to help them overcome their distrust of instruments such as mutual funds, explaining to them the impacts of inflation and how they can ensure their money is not eroded with time.

Discuss how investing a modest amount regularly, such as ₹1,000 per month, can accumulate and lead to significant savings over the years.

Practical Implementation

Step 1: Enrolling in Government Insurance Schemes

Assist them in enrolling for PMSBY and PMJJBY. Guide them through the process, ensuring they understand the benefits and how these schemes can provide a safety net. This may be easier for you, if you have a laptop with an internet connection, than it is for them. Taking that time will make a huge difference in the other person's life.

Step 2: Investing in Mutual Funds

Educate them about mutual funds and help them set up investments. You will need to help them create a Demat account and explain to them how it works, so that they can access their investment information on their own. Start with a feasible amount and gradually increase it annually. Offer support by contributing on their behalf or matching their investments if needed.

You can also guide them through fund selection and explain the incremental contribution strategy for wealth accumulation. Also explain the power of compounding and how they should avoid accessing the funds they have set aside for long-term gains.

From there, you can try to help them whenever they have any questions regarding their finances and try to introduce to more instruments for investment, such as stocks.

Creating Accessible Learning Resources

Simplify financial literacy materials or conduct workshops specifically tailored to their needs. Use visual aids and real-life scenarios to make concepts relatable. For example, you can create a booklet with basic financial terms, investment options and simple saving tips that they can refer to whenever needed.

Encourage interaction among the staff. Organise group discussions or meetings where they can share their experiences and learn from each other. This is especially possible if you live in a society or colony—this can become one of the endeavours taken up by your association.

Empowering our domestic staff with financial knowledge and opportunities is not just a social responsibility, it's an investment in their future and ours. By extending our guidance and support, we can collectively create a more financially secure and empowered society.

Remember, if you need additional guidance or support on empowering your domestic staff financially, you can connect with us at WICCI Financial Literacy & Management Council or at www.financiallysmart.in. Together, let's drive more women in India to be financially smart.

Let's join hands to drive financial literacy among women in India, spreading ripples of happiness through education, empowerment and economic independence.

The World of Business Finance: Insights for Women Entrepreneurs

'The question isn't who is going to let me; it's who is going to stop me.'

—Ayn Rand

As we conclude our exploration of personal finance, let's take a peek into the realm of business finance—a domain essential for aspiring women entrepreneurs and professionals alike. Let's unravel the challenges, myths and essential insights that women encounter as they venture into entrepreneurship or consider starting their own ventures. Let's also touch upon the basics of business finance, shedding light on key topics that women need to be aware of to navigate the financial landscape successfully.

Understanding Financial Statements

Navigating financial statements is a critical skill for entrepreneurs, as they give valuable insights into the financial health and performance of their businesses. The primary financial statements that entrepreneurs should be familiar with are:

- *Income statement*: Also known as the profit and loss statement, the income statement showcases a company's revenues, expenses and profits over a specific period. Entrepreneurs analyse this statement to assess their business's profitability and operational efficiency.
- *Balance sheet*: The balance sheet presents a snapshot of a company's financial position at a given point in time, detailing its assets, liabilities and equity. Entrepreneurs use the balance sheet to evaluate their business's financial strength, liquidity and solvency.
- *Cash flow statement*: This statement tracks the inflow and outflow of cash and cash equivalents during a specified period, providing insights into a company's cash generation and utilisation. Entrepreneurs rely on the cash flow statement to manage their business cash flow effectively and ensure liquidity.

The primary objectives of analysing financial statements are as follows:

- *Assessing profitability*: Entrepreneurs analyse income statements to determine whether their businesses are generating profits and identify areas for improving profitability.
- *Evaluating financial health*: By examining balance sheets, entrepreneurs assess their businesses' financial position, including liquidity, solvency and overall stability.

- *Managing cash flow*: Cash flow statements help entrepreneurs understand their businesses' cash flow dynamics, enabling them to forecast cash needs, manage working capital and make informed financial decisions.

Women entrepreneurs often face unique challenges and misconceptions in the business world. From gender biases and access to funding to balancing work–life responsibilities, navigating these hurdles requires resilience, determination and strategic financial management.

As women entrepreneurs step into the world of business finance, understanding financial statements and their implications is essential for success. By mastering the basics of business finance and addressing the challenges they may encounter, women can chart a path towards financial empowerment and entrepreneurial excellence. Stay tuned for our upcoming books and courses on financially smart entrepreneurs, where we'll delve into practical strategies and expert advice to help women thrive in the world of entrepreneurship.

Self-Care and Personal Happiness—Don't Think You Are Indispensable

In life, we often find ourselves deeply entrenched in the roles we play—whether as caregivers, professionals or pillars of support for our families. We believe our presence is indispensable, essential to the functioning of our homes and the happiness of our loved ones. Yet, the story of my dear friend Priya serves as a poignant reminder of the fragility of this belief.

Priya was a remarkable woman who, at the age of forty-five, tragically passed away just days after celebrating her birthday.

She had dedicated herself tirelessly to her family's well-being—managing the household, nurturing her children's education and caring for her aging parents-in-law. Despite her unwavering dedication, she often felt unappreciated and taken for granted. 'My house needs my time,' she would say. 'No one understands how much I do.'

After Priya's sudden passing, I reached out to her husband to offer support. What I discovered was both heartbreaking and eye-opening. He had quickly adapted to life without her physical presence, hiring help to manage the responsibilities she once shouldered alone. He had even relocated to reduce his travel and engaged in social activities, reclaiming a semblance of normalcy.

Priya's story is not just about the void left by her absence but also about the profound lesson it imparts. We are not indispensable. Despite our best efforts and sacrifices, life goes on without us. It underscores the importance of valuing ourselves, making time for our own happiness and nurturing our well-being.

In sharing Priya's story, I hope to inspire all women to reflect on their own lives. Remember, while our roles may be significant, our well-being and happiness are equally essential. Let's honour ourselves by nurturing our spirits, fostering meaningful connections and living lives that are rich with purpose and joy.

Action Points

- *Self-care is non-negotiable*: Prioritise 'me time' to recharge and rejuvenate.
- *Seek balance*: Don't let responsibilities overshadow your personal needs and passions.
- *Value yourself*: Your worth isn't defined by how much you do for others.
- *Support networks*: Lean on friends and loved ones for mutual support and encouragement.
- *Live with purpose*: Embrace life fully, pursuing what brings you joy and fulfilment.

Epilogue
Scripting Your Financial Success as a Financially Smart Woman

'Success is not the key to happiness. Happiness is the key to success. If you love what you are doing, you will be successful.'
—Albert Schweitze

Dear Financially Smart Women,

As we conclude this transformative journey, let's embrace the power of knowledge and the potential for financial empowerment that lies within each of us. Picture this as a friendly chat, where we share insights, stories and a vision for a future where you are not just readers but Financially Smart Women, ready to shape your destiny.

In the opening sections, we delved into the fundamentals, exploring real-life stories, scenarios and case studies. These narratives aren't just entertaining—they are profound lessons.

Dive into them; let the experiences of others become your guiding lights on this financial journey.

Remember, learning is a journey without an endpoint. Life evolves, and so should your financial knowledge. Engage, enrol in courses and upskill yourself. Be curious, be proactive, because the more you know, the more empowered you become.

In the financial realm, it's not just about how much money you earn; it's about how much you keep, save and invest. As your income rises, mastering money management becomes crucial. The SMART Life Automated Accounting System we explored earlier is your ally. Discipline and consistency are your keys to financial success.

Regardless of your income, without mastering money management, you might find yourself back at square one. Discipline and consistency, woven into your financial routine, ensure that you not only accumulate wealth but also preserve and grow it over time.

The case studies and stories shared here are not mere anecdotes—they are glimpses into the real-life financial scripts of individuals. Learn from their triumphs, understand their challenges and adapt their strategies to your unique journey. Real life may not unfold like a reel, but the principles of financial smartness remain constant.

As you journey towards financial empowerment, remember—this is uniquely yours. Each step you take, every financial decision you make, contributes to your personal narrative. Don't hesitate to seek advice, share your experiences and draw guidance from the community.

Closing this chapter, realise that you are now a Financially Smart Woman. You hold the key to your financial destiny. Embrace this role with confidence, knowing that your journey has the potential to inspire others.

Epilogue

Spring into action with the knowledge you've gained, the tools at your disposal and the community that supports you. Share your learnings, engage with others, and let's collectively build a tribe of Financially Smart Women.

Cheers to your financial journey and the road ahead!

Your financial journey is a tale of empowerment waiting to be written. May your story be one of resilience, growth and financial wisdom. As you close this chapter, consider it not an end but the beginning of a new and empowered phase of your life.

With financial savvy and camaraderie,
Nita

Acknowledgments

I EXTEND MY DEEPEST GRATITUDE TO MY DEAR HUSBAND, PRAVEEN Menezes, who has been my rock and steadfast support. He is more than a friend, and I am truly blessed to have him in my life. His unwavering encouragement and belief in me have transformed my life for the better, supporting me in all my endeavours.

To my son, Keegan Menezes, whose love, care and support have been invaluable. He has been my cheerleader, my critic and a constant source of inspiration, always boosting my aspirations. Together, Praveen and Keegan have been my biggest cheerleaders and unwavering pillars of support.

To my mother, Mrs Lany Menezes, whose saving habits and meticulous way of managing finances have been a profound inspiration. Her dedication to saving and her constant support, especially when I am caught up between work and home, have shaped my approach significantly.

To my father, (Late) Mr Sylvester Menezes who watches over me from above, showering his blessings on me. My deepest thanks to my dear sister Mrs Nancy Duarte and brother-in-law Mr Crispino Duarte, who always stood by me in my initial years and have supported me in every way.

I am also immensely grateful to my mother-in-law, Mrs Philomena Menezes whose steadfast support has been a comforting presence over the years.

A big thank you to my extended family for their continuous support.

To my cherished friends and mentors, thank you for believing in me, shaping my thoughts and illuminating my path with your invaluable guidance.

I deeply appreciate the team members at WICCI Financial Literacy and Management Council, whose dedication and collaboration have enriched my work beyond measure.

A heartfelt thank you to all my well-wishers, clients and colleagues who have supported and encouraged me over the years. Your belief in me has been a driving force in my journey.

A special acknowledgment to my LinkedIn family, whose unwavering support and encouragement have been a constant source of strength.

To my publishers and the wonderful team at Westland, especially Karthika and Aurodeep, for their incredible support and guidance.

Lastly, heartfelt gratitude to all those who shared their stories, allowing me to reach out to the world through this book and make a meaningful difference.

Nita Menezes
✉ finsmartwomen@gmail.com
🌐 http://www.financiallysmart.in/

www.ingramcontent.com/pod-product-compliance
Lightning Source LLC
Chambersburg PA
CBHW071305140726
47996CB00005B/1633